When Money Is Not Enough

Fulfillment
in work

When Money Is Not Enough

Fulfillment in work

Eileen R. Hannegan, M.S.

BEYOND
WORDS
Publishing
I N C

Beyond Words Publishing, Inc.
4443 NE Airport Road
Hillsboro, Oregon 97124-6074
503-693-8700
1-800-284-9673

Illustrations: Rusty Broderick
Graphics: Post Haste Publishing
Cover design: Principia Graphica
Interior layout: The Typesmith

Printed in the United States of America
Distributed to the book trade by Publishers Group West

The Business of Life Series
When Money Is Not Enough
You Can Have It All
Hindsights
The Woman's Book of Creativity
The Venture Adventure

Library of Congress Cataloging-in-Publication Data

Hannegan, Eileen R.
     When money is not enough : fulfillment in work / Eileen R.
  Hannegan. — [Rev. ed.]
        p.   cm. — (Business of life)
     Includes bibliographical references.
     ISBN 1-885223-14-5 : $10.95
       1. Work and family.   2. Codependency.   3. Interpersonal relations.
  I. Title.   II. Series.
  HD4904.25.H36   1995
  650.1'3—dc20   94-44136
                                                                  CIP

Dedication

This book is dedicated to the men and women who are courageous in unraveling and resolving the mystery of co-dependency in their personal and professional lives, believing that wholeness, balance and personal fulfillment can be a reality in all facets of daily living.

This book is for every organization that is committed to providing the healthiest work environment for its employees, while trusting that bottom-line results will reflect that commitment.

This book is for every working person who wants his or her job to be an extension and expression of self that adds value to the community and supports him/her in a quality lifestyle.

This book is dedicated to providing insights, techniques, strategies and innovative systems that assist employees, organizations and consultants in establishing and maintaining healthy work environments that break the cycle of dysfunction and co-dependency.

Table of Contents

Disclaimer

All of the cases and examples I refer to actually
occurred and are accurately represented. However, I have changed the names, locations and
identifying details to protect the privacy of the
individuals involved.

Acknowledgments

A special thanks to Nancy Lynch, who supported the vision of this book and encouraged me in the months of labor to bring it to birth.

To Kim Cook, who mentored me in the work and creativity of becoming a writer, I express my deep appreciation for her humor and drive.

I would like to thank my clients, students and colleagues, who cheered me on through the high and low times, keeping the vision bright.

I offer a most sincere thank you to Rusty Broderick, whose devotion, support and hard work, mixed with his refreshing humor, gave me constant encouragement and inspiration during the writing of this book.

My daughter Brenna's understanding and support was a breath of fresh air during long periods of separation due to my work and the writing of this book. Her constant refrain, "Mom, I know you can do it," and going together to matinees on Sunday afternoons kept me balanced and refreshed during this time of growth and transformation.

Drawing Exercise

Yourself at Work

Before you begin to read this book, take a few moments to draw a picture of yourself at work.

As you draw this picture, practice being aware of how you are *feeling* during this exercise, as well as the reactions in your body.

As you look at the picture of yourself at work, answer these questions:

1. What is the title of this picture? _____

_____

_____

2. How does this picture make me feel? _____

_____

_____

_____

3. What is the best part about this picture? _____

_____

_____

_____

4. What is missing from this picture? _____

_____

_____

_____

5. What are my bodily reactions to this picture? _____

_____

_____

_____

6. Is this picture of myself at work really who I am? _____

_____

_____

_____

7. Do I:

Love my work? _____

Like my work? _____

Just do my work? _____

Dislike my work? _____

Hate my work? _____

8. What would I like to eliminate in my work? _____

_____

_____

_____

_____

_____

9. What would I like to keep in my work? _____

_____

_____

_____

_____

_____

_____

10. What percentage of my work is an expression of my real self? _____

_____

_____

_____

_____

_____

_____

Yourself at Home

Now draw a picture of yourself at home.

As you draw this picture, again practice being aware of how you are *feeling* during this exercise. Also, remember to be aware of your bodily reactions.

As you look at the picture of yourself at home, answer these questions:

1. What is the title of this picture? _____

_____

_____

2. How does this picture make me feel? _____

_____

_____

_____

3. What is the best part about this picture? _____

_____

_____

_____

4. What is missing from this picture? _____

_____

_____

_____

5. What are my bodily reactions to this picture? _____

_____

_____

_____

6. Is this picture of myself really who I am? _____

_____

_____

_____

7. Do I:

Love myself? _____

Like myself? _____

Put up with myself? _____

Dislike myself? _____

Hate myself? _____

8. What would I like to eliminate in myself? _____

_____

_____

_____

_____

9. What do I like and want to keep as part of me? _____

_____

_____

_____

_____

10. What percentage of my living is an authentic expression of the real me? _____

_____

_____

_____

Now, compare and contrast the person in each of the pictures.

1. How are they alike? _____

_____

_____

2. How do they differ? _____

_____

_____

3. Where do I feel most comfortable? _____

_____

_____

_____

4. Where do I feel most alive? _____

_____

_____

_____

5. List the positive aspects of both pictures:

Myself at Work	*Myself*
_____	_____
_____	_____
_____	_____
_____	_____
_____	_____
_____	_____
_____	_____

6. List the negative aspects of both pictures:

Myself at Work	*Myself*
_____	_____
_____	_____
_____	_____
_____	_____
_____	_____
_____	_____
_____	_____

7. Is there a common theme that is expressed in both pictures? What is it? _____

_____

_____

_____

8. What are three things that would give me more satisfaction in my work?

1._____

_____

2._____

_____

3._____

_____

9. What are three things that would give me more satisfaction in my life?

1._____

_____

2._____

_____

3._____

_____

10. On a scale of 1-10, do I experience fulfillment in my work?

No Fulfillment   Definite Fulfillment

1 ----------------------------- 5 ----------------------------- 10

11. On a scale of 1-10, do I experience contentment in my life?

No Contentment   Definite Contentment

1 ----------------------------- 5 ----------------------------- 10

Introduction

Making the Pieces Fit

In 1983 I was one of the first alcohol/drug counselors in the United States to provide community education and support groups for Adult Children of Alcoholics. Claudia Black's book, *It Will Never Happen to Me!*, had launched the movement of Adult Children of Alcoholics (ACOA) seeking recovery for themselves. The word *co-dependency* started to gain serious attention.

I was a bit confused in those days. This information applied so well to my own struggles with co-dependency, yet my parents did not abuse alcohol or drugs.

Even though I did not officially belong to ACOA, I worked well with this group and could identify with the issues it addressed for its members. I secretly believed that co-dependency had far-reaching effects into other family dynamics that were not necessarily affected by alcohol or drugs.

As my personal and professional journey continued, I decided to pursue my education in organizational behavior with a master's degree in organizational development. It was like watching an old familiar movie with new actors: I kept seeing the same dynamics in the dysfunctional family played out in organizational analysis. Using dysfunctional family systems as my model, I was continually right on target identifying the root problems of the organization. My teachers were thrilled with my results but apprehensive about my model. Soon I realized that maybe it wasn't such a good idea to let them in on my "fail-proof method."

The fail-proof method was simple and accurate. I was baffled that other people weren't figuring it out. I became very hopeful when Anne Wilson Schaef's book, *The Addictive Organization*, pointed out some aspects of dysfunction and addiction in the workplace.

To take this issue a step further, an organization's dysfunction is on a much larger and common ground when one focuses on co-dependency and counterdependency in the workplace. This is where root issues of dysfunction can be identified accurately.

As we enter the 1990s, the gospel of co-dependency has been spread by John Bradshaw and others. Their testimony states that most families and society as a whole are permeated with co-dependency and dysfunction.

The business community is beginning to show genuine interest in resolving dysfunctional issues by establishing healthy work environments.

Many employees are also beginning to deal with co-dependency issues in their personal and professional lives.

A career choice is now seriously assessed in terms of its personal fulfillment by the person who is resolving co-dependency issues.

Quality of life is realized by those who resolve co-dependency and dysfunctional issues in their personal lives. Their next crucial step is to bring that same quality of life into their career and work environment.

This book is a product of 16 years of counseling and consulting with individuals and organizations dealing with these critical issues.

Chapter 1

When the Self Is Lost

Co-dependency—what is it and where does it come from? The concept has come into the forefront of today's society as a buzzword that has aroused much interest. Co-dependency was first given attention some 30 years ago in the alcohol-recovery field.

In the alcohol/drug recovery field, dependency refers to someone who is dependent on alcohol or other drugs. A co-dependent is a person whose focus is on a dependent person—either a parent, family member, spouse, child or loved one.

Since the emergence of Adult Children of Alcoholics, co-dependency has taken on an expanded definition.

Co-dependency has moved beyond the relationship with the alcohol/drug-affected dysfunctional family system. It now relates also to co-dependents who are raised in homes where alcohol or drug abuse is *not* present. In Robert Subby's book, *Lost in the Shuffle: The Co-dependent Reality*, and Ann Wilson Schaef's book, *Co-Dependence: Misunderstood-Mistreated*, a broader definition of co-dependency has emerged.

Co-dependency now includes any person raised in a dysfunctional family system who has experienced chronic loss of self. Co-dependency is often an unconscious state. Co-dependent men and women look to other people, authorities, and social and religious rules to define their own identity.

Simply stated, a co-dependent person's self-image and way of looking at life is defined by other people. His focus is outside of himself, primarily on authority figures, for validation, self-esteem and self-worth. A co-dependent person is not in touch with who he is as an individual. He is not aware of his wants and needs, nor is he aware of how to meet his needs.

THE FAMILY INFLUENCE

The belief system of a person's family sets him up to be co-dependent. If the family is authoritarian or has rigid religious, military or ethnic influences, co-dependent beliefs and behaviors are reinforced. The co-dependent person believes there is only one right way to live life.

Even in a family free of chemical and physical abuse, co-dependency can be established. Society fortifies these same co-dependent beliefs and behaviors. The family and social system that reinforces co-dependent behavior denies the cultivation and validation of the individual. The value of her person, her gifts, her talents and her view of life is neither developed nor allowed to grow. Co-dependency is reinforced by systems that regiment a person's perception of herself, society and the way she lives her life.

Robert Subby states, "Co-dependency is a pattern of living, coping, and problem solving created and maintained by a set of dysfunctional rules within a family or social system. These rules interfere with healthy growth and make constructive change very difficult, if not impossible."

These rules have power since the belief is that there is only one way—the right way. The person raised in this system realizes that if he strays from following the rules, he will be rejected as a person. If he conforms to the rules, he will be accepted as a person. Outside performance is valued, and inward conviction is constricted, repressed and invalidated.

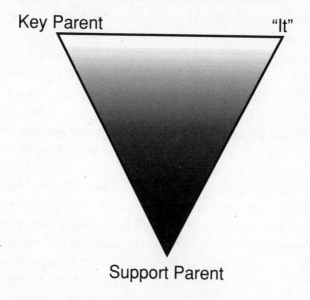

Key Parent   "It"

Support Parent

A dysfunctional family system focuses on the Key Parent (or the addicted parent). Addiction relates not only to alcohol or drugs, but also to many other addictions that distort a family dynamic. These include religious addiction, gambling, compulsive eating, compulsive buying and even work addiction. Whatever the addiction, the Key Parent focuses on the "It" of addiction. The Support Parent does everything possible to make the "It" work for the Key Parent.

FAMILY IDENTITY FORMATS

I have worked with many co-dependent adults who have experienced the same dysfunctional family system, in a variety of Family Identity Formats. The following is a list I have compiled:

1. *Idealized American Family.* This family follows all the traditions and practices of the idealized family: Parents are loving, and children are cared for. There is family participation in school and church activities and demonstration of affection and attention that is sincere though superficial. The family members know their roles and follow them accordingly.

2. *Ethnic Family.* A strong ethnic influence is the first impression of this type of family. Before much time passes in conversation, one is clear about the heritage of this family. The ethnic influence is woven into most conversation. Viewpoints are either accepted or rejected according to the ethnic principles. Some examples of typical comments include: "Oh, I couldn't spend that much money. You know how the Scottish are." "Well, being a hard-headed German, I'm going to need some convincing." "Oh, yes, being Irish does give me the gift of gab." Female and male roles are strongly influenced by the ethnic heritage in these families and are handed down from generation to generation. To stray from the ethnic way is to oppose one's own family.

3. *Robot Family.* This family goes through the right moves at home, work and church. Affection is not displayed. Positive and negative emotions are not expressed. It is a monotonous, predictable way of life. *Star Trek's* Mr. Spock would have done quite well in this identity format.

4. *Physical Disability in the Family.* The disability becomes the "It" in this identity format. The family members cope with dysfunctional dynamics when a disability is the identity of the family. Conversations reflect this focus: "Since my mother is disabled I have decided not to go to college." "I would never be able to travel out of the state because of my brother's health." "He is very demanding, but it is because of his illness."

5. *Mental Illness in the Family.* Like a physical disability, a mental illness can be the "It" in a dysfunctional family, especially when the mental illness is not acknowledged or dealt with properly. Many of these families are in denial about the mental illness, as are families affected by alcoholism. Crazy behavior is treated as normal. Reality is severely distorted in this identity format.

6. *Military Family.* All the family members wear invisible uniforms 24 hours a day. The family unit is the extension of the branch of service. Family rules and regulations agree with military standards. The family does not have an identity outside of the service. This becomes particularly apparent when the parent retires from the military. Without the rank and position in a military culture, the identity format is severely shaken.

7. *Religious Family.* Conforming to the image and likeness of the church is the strong "It" of this identity format, with the added reinforcement that encouraging conformity is "being right with God." No one wants to be wrong with God, so this added incentive is hard to resist. If you rebel against this family, you go against God Himself. Family members are caught between being true to self and going against God. The family will use "God's way" to manipulate the behaviors of all the members. Incredible amounts of guilt are inflicted upon anyone who would question "God's way," according to this family.

What all these families have in common is that the individual is *not* groomed and supported in his or her identity. Family members conform to the Family Identity Format and take on co-dependent roles in order to function in dysfunction.

A healthy family identity first cultivates and affirms each member's individual identity. Second, each family identity

should incorporate the influences of ethnic culture, militar
service, etc., without losing personal identity.

ROLES

In a dysfunctional family system, the Key Parent focuses o
the "It," and the Support Parent focuses on both the "It" an
on the Key Parent. The children develop survival roles in orde
to cope with the situation.

These roles help the children survive a dysfunctional sys
tem and groom them in co-dependency.

Miniparent

Usually, the oldest child is the Miniparent. Miniparent
parent the parents. They help and save everyone because the
believe it is their duty. If they don't take on the responsibilit
the fear is too great: "Who knows what will happen?" Th
Miniparent also takes care of the younger siblings. Thes
children sometimes run a household because the parents ar
incapacitated. The Key Parent is obsessed with the "It." Th
Key Parent is "under the influence" of the "It." The Suppor
Parent is "under the influence" of the Key Parent.

Troublemaker

The second child is usually the Troublemaker. Th
Troublemaker acts out whatever tension is in the househol
The dysfunctional household reflects an image that everythin
is fine, everything is wonderful: "We don't have any problems.
The household looks fine from the outside, but there is a prob
lem. In the family, the focus is on the Troublemaker—the chil
who is acting out, has bad grades and is a discipline problem a
school. The family says, "If only we could get this kid fixe
then the family would be fine."

In structured, militaristic, authoritarian or religious house
holds, everyone else is proper, good, right, clean and polishe

The Troublemaker looks like the problem. This child takes the brunt of the dysfunction that exists in the household.

Commonly, when the Miniparent goes off to college or gets married, the Troublemaker moves into the position of Miniparent.

Shadow

The third child is usually the Shadow. The parents are pre-occupied, the Miniparent is busy being good, and the Trouble-maker is busy being in trouble. The Shadow avoids confrontation at all costs. This child avoids all attention, both positive and negative. His role is the "no role" role. I find that the Shadow person has the most difficulty in attempting to define self. The other roles at least define positive or negative characteristics that have been developed in the role definition. The Shadow child is defined by a void.

Tension Breaker

The Tension Breaker deals with the tension in the household by becoming the family clown. He jokes to take the attention off the issue. He will do whatever it takes—sing or dance, if necessary—to get the pressure diverted to himself. If the anxiety starts to heighten, he immediately calls attention to himself to break the tension. He sacrifices himself to offset the family tension and acts as a peacemaker by jumping in the middle of the tension.

REINFORCEMENT OF CO-DEPENDENCY BY FAMILY, RELIGION AND SOCIETY

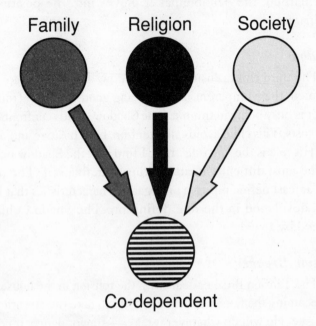

Family, religion and society have worked together to reinforce co-dependency by sending messages to the child what to think, how to act, what to do and how to do it. Therefore, the child conforms to the messages and becomes co-dependent. Co-dependent beliefs and behaviors are reinforced. The child becomes co-dependent instead of becoming a unique individual with a strong, secure identity.

Parental authority has sent us messages: "This is how you behave as a child in this household." If you conform, you are accepted; if you don't, you're rejected. The child does not want to be rejected, so he conforms.

Society has done a good job of sending co-dependent messages to all of us. Society has sent messages telling us how to act, how to behave in society, what's acceptable and what's unacceptable. This starts in the educational system and extends into the workplace.

Religion (not true spirituality) has been another strong influence that sends us instructions on how to please God or receive His wrath, all based on our performance of "dos" and "don'ts" without consideration for our personal convictions. Father Leo Booth's book, *When God Becomes a Drug: Breaking the Chains of Religious Addiction and Abuse*, addresses the issue of religious addiction that promotes co-dependency by "using God, the Bible and people in a negative and destructive way."

These major influences teach the child what makes a "good person." Black-and-white rules of how the child should behave are reinforced over and over again.

Most people have not been raised in a home environment that validates who they are to themselves. Children are raised in home environments that teach them to perform, conform and behave. So, when these children become adults, they conform, instead of knowing who they really are, what their needs are and how to meet those needs. Today's co-dependent adult feels overwhelming guilt about having needs. He learns to ignore his needs and to not be selfish. He must do the "right thing." He is prepared to conform to what others want, which sets him up for career frustration, corporate burnout and an unfulfilled life.

Chapter 2

Who Defines My Career?

EFFECTS ON CAREER SATISFACTION

Usually our career choices are formulated from the messages and impressions we receive from parents, religion, the educational system and society. The way we approach our careers is formulated long before we realize we have career choices and options. Most of us have chosen jobs according to our co-dependency influence, rather than choosing careers according to who we are as people and what fulfills us.

Society and the educational system evaluate career choice according to aptitudes in math, reading skills, intelligence level and work history. The focus of the person as an individual has just recently been recognized as an important factor. Careers have been regulated by what society dictates as the "open job market" or what jobs we are able to secure within our work history and educational background.

It is extremely important to note that there are two sides of a career. One side is the person's development of her individual identity, taking into account her interests, natural ability, values and motivations. The second side of career is the practical side—the development of skills, training, education and experience. These are all pieces of the puzzle that work together in laying the foundation for moving beyond co-dependency issues.

Co-dependency influences a person's view of life according to the black-and-white rules that she grew up with in her family of origin and that were reinforced by society's influence.

Co-dependency can be a fraudulent identity that a person assumes from shaping himself according to others' perceptions.

It is crucial that co-dependency issues be resolved in order that an individual can become integrated with her true self. In the self-discovery experience, a career identity will be realized and personal fulfillment can occur.

Career identity means a person comes into an integrated identity. The extension of true self in the career world is career identity. It's not a suit you put on, a mask you wear or a position you fill each day. Career identity is the extension of who you are in the work environment, not just what you do.

I do not believe that people can come into their true career identities unless they first discover who they are as unique individuals. This is done by dealing with childhood pain, anger and life's disappointments, by working through co-dependency issues that keep us from discovering our true selves. We must identify our needs and our wants, and learn the skills to live integrated lives. We must match our true selves and career identities to find fulfillment by blending these elements into one complete person.

In other words, most of us have not been validated in our identity, nor have we been encouraged to expand and explore who we are. Therefore, it is important that co-dependency issues be resolved and self-identity be established in order for career identity to become a reality in one's life. Otherwise, a person will unconsciously keep repeating co-dependent/counterdependent work relationships, which ultimately leads to career burnout.

CAREER BURNOUT

Career stress and *burnout* are key words that are heard often in today's business community. Even employees satisfied in their career choice and job positions find career burnout has become a reality due to unresolved and unconscious co-dependency issues.

Career stresses are magnified and reinforced by co-dependent beliefs and behaviors in the workplace. For the overextended co-dependent employee, without boundaries to protect and nurture self, career burnout is inevitable.

Underlying co-dependency issues must be resolved to reduce stress and avoid burnout. If a person changes jobs or careers to lessen the stress, and the co-dependent issues are not resolved, the cycle will continue.

Co-dependent employees are disconnected from themselves. If they do not discover their true selves first, they will never find their true career identities. They will continue the vicious cycle of career frustration, stress and burnout until they deal with their co-dependency issues.

Signs and Symptoms of Burnout

Physical

Disrupted sleep patterns
Fluctuations in weight and/or appetite problems
Exhaustion, physically worn out
Health problems
Disinterest in sexual activities
Increased use of nicotine, alcohol or other drugs
Decrease in exercise and physical self-care

Emotional and Behavioral

Emotional exhaustion
Chronic depression

Holding on to anger and resentment
Heightened anxiety
Sense of isolation and feeling alone
Feeling a lack of purpose and no direction
Inability to relax
Negative attitudes and opinions
Impulsive behavior with no regard for outcome
Loss of control with emotional/physical outbursts

Family and Social

Increased time spent away from home and family
Loss of interest in family activities
Short temper with family members
Inability to enjoy family vacations
Difficulty in enjoying time with friends
Increased isolation
Increased use of television to escape interaction with family
Perceived lack of support from religious beliefs and practices
Overwhelming stress in combination of major life change, birth, death(s), financial loss, divorce or loss of significant other

Work

Chronic tardiness and leaving early
Increased use of sick leave and vacation leave
Increased tendency to distract easily and waste time
Inability to complete work tasks consistently
Loss of attention and ability to deal with clients' problems
Decreased job satisfaction without effort to make changes
Growing resentment and anger toward clients, co-workers, company or supervisor
Feelings of entrapment with no options

ARE YOU ON YOUR WAY TO BURNING OUT?

Answer the following questions by reviewing your life at home and work. Rate how often these symptoms are true for you.

1 = Rare 2 = Sometimes 3 = Often 4 = Frequently 5 = Usually

_____ 1. I have trouble sleeping.

_____ 2. I use alcohol and/or drugs to feel better.

_____ 3. I feel worn out even when I get adequate sleep.

_____ 4. My physical self-care is not up to par.

_____ 5. I have no interest in sexual activities.

_____ 6. I feel I have no real purpose in life.

_____ 7. Even though I am exhausted, I can't relax.

_____ 8. I feel sad for no reason.

_____ 9. I withdraw from family and friends.

_____ 10. I feel overwhelmed by life.

_____ 11. I am irritated with others.

_____ 12. Social activities are draining.

_____ 13. I feel helpless to change my situation.

_____ 14. I feel alone and unsupported.

_____ 15. I work hard but accomplish little.

_____ 16. I feel unable to deal with others' problems.

_____ 17. I feel sick.

_____ 18. My eating habits are inappropriate.

_____ 19. I am not in control of my emotions.

_____ 20. I feel like "What's the use anyway?"

Score:

20-40   You're maintaining balance.

41-60   Take some preventive action to stay in balance.

61-80   You're on the edge of burnout.

81-100   You're in burnout.

THE CAREER RECOVERY PROCESS

Career recovery is an eight-stage process. This process breaks down dysfunctional/co-dependent beliefs and behaviors while establishing the individual's personal and professional identity. These are the stages that are necessary to attain personal identity, authentic career expression and personal fulfillment.

1. *Denial.* The individual's refusal or resistance to acknowledge the present job position is causing emotional and physical disruption. The person is in the vicious cycle of co-dependency and dysfunctional beliefs and behaviors. These issues continually frustrate his life. No matter how hard people in this stage try, they cannot seem to find the answers in the same old way of reacting to life.

   People in this stage, even when confronted with the co-dependency issues that are keeping them in this dysfunctional cycle, will choose not to hear the information. They will continue to choose jobs and work environments that will set them up for frustration, failure, stress and burnout.

2. *Discomfort.* People in this stage realize that something is not quite right, but they are not sure what. They are aware of some negative things that are happening in the work environment. They start looking at others' jobs and asking, "Why can't I have a job like that?"

   As in Denial, they think there are no options or choices, so they continue to maintain the status quo. They begin to feel discomfort, enough to consider that there may be another way out of the situation.

3. *Confrontation.* At the confrontation stage, people start to say, "This job, career or work environment no longer works for me, and it is time to make a change." They are not sure how that change should come about. They do realize that if there isn't a radical change in the job or environment, they have no choice but to make a change themselves. They list

the positives and negatives of the job. The positives do not outweigh the fear of making a change. Vacillating between whether to stay or leave continues because of fear and uncertainty.

4. *Inward Conviction.* This is a reflection stage. People look inside at what has and hasn't worked for them in their past career choices. They begin self-discovery and realize what events, people and places occurred in their lives to bring them to where they are today. They confront personal illusions and self-promises that have frustrated them in their career lives. It is also the time when people say they need a job, career and work environment that completes their lives instead of dividing themselves into segments.

5. *Self-Resolution.* In this phase, people have resolved many co-dependency issues and surround themselves with healthy, supportive people to gain self-identity and self-esteem. Out of self-identity, a strengthened self-esteem starts to emerge. Career clarification and career direction begin to formulate.

People start to believe they have what it takes. They believe they possess skills and abilities to gain meaningful employment. They are willing to emotionally walk through their fears to gain whatever training or education the career change requires. The established true self is accompanied by inward validation. Belief in self begins to fortify them in their quest for discovery of true self and career identity.

6. *Connecting.* Confidence to promote oneself in a chosen career field arrives at the Connecting stage. Inward validation tells people who they are, what the suitable work environment is and the career direction they need to feel complete. They settle for nothing less than to be in a supportive environment with people doing work that is worthwhile to them. They connect with healthy people and a positive work environment that is according to their true self and career identity.

7. *Personal Purpose*. At this stage, people have deep, inner experiences of their true selves. They clearly see their true selves and career identities. They extend the focus of self and become more aware of their role in the universal picture, experiencing the extension of themselves to others. They experience self-contentment. Creative energy begins to flow and increased emotional and spiritual strength is experienced. This newly found strength helps them create and respond to both personal and professional issues in their lives.

They finally learn to look for ways to give meaning to life (proactive) instead of expecting life to provide meaning (passive). They are free to speak and express their own purpose in life, secure in their ideas and thoughts. This true self/career identity brings them to Personal Purpose, which is in accordance with Spiritual Wholeness.

8. *Spiritual Wholeness*. This is the result of the career recovery process, which integrates the true self, career identity and personal purpose—the inside matches the outside. They are in tune with their Higher Self/Higher Power. Their daily life reflects an inward knowingness of being right with self and spiritual path, and they are personally fulfilled in all areas of their life.

REMOVING EMOTIONAL BLOCKS

In career recovery, emotional blocks need to be identified and dealt with. The following are some of the major emotional blocks that co-dependent people need to resolve in pursuing their personal and career identities:

1. *Feeling Feelings*. Most co-dependents have been raised in a family and society that restrict feeling and the expression of feelings. Those who do not feel their feelings when events occur will never know their true selves or discover their career identities.

Co-dependent people tend to have frozen and blocked feelings. Co-dependent people need to experience, discover and identify feelings. The next step is to learn how to express those feelings appropriately. They can then exercise their feelings assertively, balancing out the extremes of passive and aggressive behavior.

2. *Anger*. Anger is usually the undercurrent of hurt, depression and sadness. Anger can stem from what has happened to us, as well as what has not happened to us. Emotional abuse or emotional neglect both can fuel unresolved anger issues.

Many co-dependent people are terrified to face their anger and talk about it. They are afraid that if they do start letting their anger out, it will consume them and everyone else.

There are numerous co-dependent people who are angry but unable to identify it. They have suppressed the anger and turned the anger on themselves instead of directing it to a parent, sibling or significant person in their lives.

Anger is multifaceted and layered. As a person deals with co-dependency issues, anger will rise to the surface. It will need to be dealt with at different levels in order to go to the next stage of recovery.

3. *Control*. This is a major issue co-dependent people need to face. Many co-dependent people are not willing to give up control because control makes them feel secure. When co-dependent people feel loss of control, their fear heightens. They become even more desperate to control, whatever the situation. Not only do they control others, but they also restrict and constrain themselves. What they don't realize is that they are restricted by trying to control others. Control is a two-sided trap. Control restricts us from living our own lives as well as not allowing others to live theirs.

4. *Guilt*. It is important to progress to a point where we can forgive ourselves for who we are and who we are not. Most of

us live under a cloud of phantom guilt that we believe in buy into. Guilt will cripple. It is a continual discounting ar discrediting of an individual who doesn't measure up to a invisible yardstick. Guilt tells us that whatever we do is *n* good enough. We have been groomed in guilt, which is th glue that keeps co-dependency intact.

5. *Shame.* Shame is a deeper discounting and discrediting self than guilt. Guilt invalidates us for what we do or don do. Shame invalidates who we are as people. The shan that some co-dependent people live with is so overwhelr ing that suicide looks like the only way out. The rejectic of self is to the core level of the person. Shame can imm bilize a person in career recovery and in finding his true se No matter the degree of shame we carry with us, it is nece sary to deal with shame in order to embrace self.

6. *Grief.* Grief involves walking through the pain and hurt what was and what wasn't. The other side of this pain releasing the pain that for years has been carried with into all areas of our lives. Until one grieves and mourns t loss, one cannot claim one's life as one's own. This gri process enables us to let go of the past and live in the no

7. *Becoming a Friend to Self.* Loving oneself and becoming friend to self is the recovery process that co-depende people need to work through. Starting a friendship and deve oping a loving bond with oneself is crucial. When we acce all the parts of who we are, we integrate our true selve embracing who we are and who we are not as well as embra ing our special qualities and our limits and shortcomings.

8. *Forgiveness.* As part of building a relationship with self, v need to address the issue of forgiving ourselves. Most c dependent people are not willing or able to forgive themselve As relationship with self increases in a supportive enviro ment, it becomes possible to forgive ourselves and others.

9. *Self-Esteem.* Developing and strengthening self-esteem is an important ingredient in breaking through the emotional blocks to attain true self and career identity. It doesn't matter how much education and training we have or how brilliantly we perform a job. Unless we strengthen our self-esteem, we will never discover who we truly are.

Low self-esteem is an important issue, since most of us haven't been encouraged to develop a strong sense of self. This doesn't mean becoming a selfish person who doesn't care about anyone else. By having a healthy self-image, we can extend ourselves authentically. We can say, "I do love myself," and extend that to others, instead of simply walking through a performance, pretending to be helpful and kind, yet resenting it.

To determine where you are with your own personal growth at this time, do this exercise. (1) Go to the mirror. (2) Look in the mirror. (3) First say to yourself (use your name), "We're in this together." Take a few moments to really see yourself. See how that feels.

Then repeat the exercise. Use your name and tell yourself, "I like you." How does that feel? Do you like you?

The real test is to tell yourself, "I love you." Use your name and say, "I love you." Can you say that to yourself? Do you love you? With practice, you'll know where you stand with yourself in the recovery process. By developing a relationship with self, your self-esteem will be strengthened.

PREPARING FOR CAREER CHANGE

In preparing for career change, there are four areas to be considered. I call them the Puzzle Pieces of Career Recovery. Each piece relates to the other, providing all the components necessary for a successful transition.

The first piece is Resolving Co-Dependency Issues. This is necessary to attain true self-image and career identity. The second piece is Exploring Career Fields by networking and informational interviewing. The third piece, Trying Out Options, exposes the person to different career possibilities through volunteer and contract services. Developing skills is the fourth puzzle piece, which focuses on education, experience and training. It is important to note that all these pieces can be worked together simultaneously in order for the puzzle to take shape. For those who tend to be overly compulsive, it is also very effective to slow down and give special attention to each piece in the order listed.

THE PUZZLE PIECES OF CAREER RECOVERY

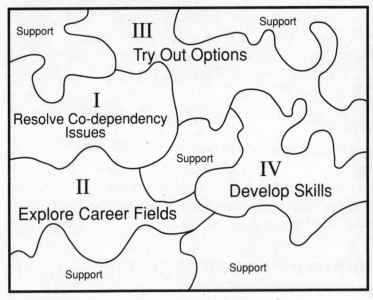

I. Resolving Co-dependency Issues

Resolving co-dependency issues is the foundation of career recovery and the key piece to your puzzle. The basic steps in resolving these issues are:

1. Mourn It
2. Face It
3. Choose It
4. Do It

Step 1. Mourn It

All of us have painful childhood memories of how we were invalidated in our upbringing by parents, siblings, relatives, clergy and teachers. Some of these painful memories are the result of needs that were not recognized and therefore ignored. By reviewing our childhood history—our roots—we will discover the pain of what it was and wasn't.

To understand the "mystery of why," it is important to investigate our past history, gather the information and mourn the painful parts.

Step 2. Face It

By reviewing our past, we can become aware of how those co-dependent beliefs and behaviors are impacting our lives today. Ask, "What are the results?" and "Do I want to continue my life like this?" We must face the issues that need to be dealt with. Let go of blaming others and holding on to excuses that promote destructive behaviors.

Step 3. Choose It

Choose it, by exploring the options that exist in a healthy way of life. By exploring options and healthy choices, we can begin to change our life/career outlook for the better. To resolve co-dependency issues, we have to change our belief systems and behavioral practices. Change comes by choosing another way.

Step 4. Do It

Implementing through practice new beliefs and behaviors into our lives is the Do It step. Most of the time, implementing new behaviors first brings new beliefs into our lives. Don't wait to believe it—"Just do it."

In my childhood, the parochial school, Sister Sylvester and my family reinforced my belief that I had better rely on my looks and personality to get through school. In other words, I didn't have the brains to do much more than maintain a "C" grade average (I hoped!) and graduate from high school. My low self-esteem reinforced my belief. My behavior as a floundering student made it my reality.

This pattern continued throughout my life and became painfully evident in my feeble career image. Of the numerous accomplishments I did achieve, few survived the co-dependent maze of self-doubt and critical invalidation.

By mourning (step 1) my past history of this issue and facing (step 2) the constant theme in my daily life, I found that it was time to change it (step 3). I began to realize that I was intelligent, and in addition to looks and personality, I did have brains. Part of the Choose It step was to ask for help in gaining the skills I needed to use my brain effectively. This took a deep commitment to self through practice and discipline.

My Do It step (step 4) was going back to college to finish my degree. This was not just scary, but terrifying. Not only was I breaking my co-dependent belief system, but I was also changing my self-image and my identity within my family of origin. The Do It step was crucial in increasing my self-esteem and career image.

Even though these four steps may sound simple, they are profound. The intensity of these steps makes it impossible to complete this process successfully without support. As shown in the illustration of the Puzzle Pieces of Career Recovery, support is what makes the puzzle come together—support by people who have worked on resolving co-dependency issues in their personal and professional lives, people whose lives reflect these changes. Support is the life source. You must be surrounded with supportive validation of who you are to yourself. Your co-dependent beliefs and behaviors that sabotage your life will also be exposed by this support.

It is important to hold on to the belief that supportive people have in you. You must hold on to this belief while you practice your new behavior. In time, the practice will become your reality.

It was because Marge, Barbara, Lou and Dick believed in me that I had the motivation to pursue my degree. I was able to walk through the terror of doing it. I held on to their belief, encouragement and support. After months of hard work going to school, working two jobs and raising two children on my own, I received my degree with a "B" average. Now the belief in myself was mine. I did have brains, but more than that I had myself. I was my own support. I was able to move on for myself and my career by accomplishing another Do It step. I went on to complete a master's degree, maintaining a "B+" average and enjoying every minute of the adventure.

II. Exploring Career Fields

The next piece of the puzzle involves exploring career fields. Investigation is the exciting part of this piece. Take it seriously, but don't take it too seriously. You're not making a commitment. You're not making drastic changes. You're simply investigating different options that sound interesting. What is exciting about exploring career fields is discovering different opportunities that are available.

Networking

Networking is a key ingredient in exploring career fields. Some people are more comfortable than others in networking, but even people who don't feel comfortable meeting others can learn to network. What networking means is people meeting people. One of my mentors, Dick W., said, "You have to keep turning over the stones." I was always trying to decide whether this statement had some deep meaning. He meant that I had to keep pursuing the leads I received in the networking process. Is it this one? Is it that one? Does this work? Does it not work? Keep turning over the stones. Some networking information will lead you on a wild-goose chase, but other leads will prove invaluable in the career-recovery process. To begin networking, start talking to friends, relatives, acquaintances and anyone you meet.

- *Tell them where you are.* "I'm in career change." "I'm considering a different career." "I'm seeing if I can be more mobile in the career field I'm in."

- *Tell them what you're looking for.* "I want a job in which I can have more mobility, more flexibility." "I want to be able to work at home." "I'm looking for a job with travel."

- *Let them know what kind of leads you're looking for.* "I'm looking for leads in the photography field." "I would like to meet with a CEO of a manufacturing company." "I would like to have you introduce me to your boss."

One of my clients was very interested in photography, yet she had limited experience. By networking she met someone who mentioned the position of photo stylist. She started asking, "What is a photo stylist? "What do they do?" "Who is a stylist I can talk to?" After gathering the information, she continued to "turn over the stones," and a year later she is loving her work as a photo stylist doing major projects in the Portland, Oregon, area.

As you "turn over your stones" in networking, keep track of these people. Fill out an index card (or a Rolodex) that is exclusively used for your networking contacts. Some people prefer a loose-leaf binder for the networking information data sheets.

Networking Information Data Sheet

Date: _____

Importance of contact: Low 1-2-3-4-5 High

Referred by: _____

Contact name: _____

   Industry: _____

   Title: _____

   Business: _____

   Address: _____

   Phone: _____

Letter of introduction: _____

   Date sent: _____

Important information: _____

_____

_____

_____

Results: Positive_____ Negative_____ Uncertain_____

Follow-up:

   Phone call: _____ Date: _____

   Meeting: _____ Date: _____

   Thank-you letter: _____ Date: _____

    With networking, you're meeting people and getting to know people. You're developing working relationships within the business community. You receive encouragement and support from people you meet while networking. You will also meet some people who are discouraging. But continue to "turn over the stones." It works!

Informational Interviews

Informational interviews are for gathering information about career fields and the different positions within the field. It's not necessarily looking for a job.

This information is to tell you the history of the career field, why it exists, if it is growing, and how is it growing. More personally, it tells you what kind of people work in this career field, what kind of training is needed, what kind of education is needed, and what the salary ranges and benefits are.

Informational Interview Sheet

Date: _____

Importance of contact: Low 1-2-3-4-5 High

Referred by: _____

Contact name: _____

   Industry: _____

   Title: _____

   Business: _____

   Address: _____

   Phone: _____

History of company: _____

_____

Other companies in this field: _____

_____

ositive aspects of field: _____

_____

Iegative aspects of field: _____

_____

uture prospects of growth: _____

_____

ypes of positions available in field: _____

_____

ducational requirements: _____

_____

kills and training requirements: _____

_____

ay scale/benefits: _____

_____

Vords of wisdom: _____

_____

equest a referral contact: _____

_____

When you're arranging an informational interview, these are
few things to remember:

1. *Introduce yourself and use the name of the person who referred you.*
   "Hello, my name is Susan Sanden, and Don Bower suggested
   I call you."

2. *Tell them where you are in your career search.* "I have 15 years
   of experience in sales. I feel my background and training
   would be transferable to your field."

3. *Tell the person the reason for your contact.* "I was hoping to
   interview you in order to gather the information necessary
   to consider a career change. Your feedback would be most
   helpful in clearly defining the opportunities in this field."

4. *Ask the person if you could meet for 20-30 minutes.* Be respect
ful of the interviewer's time. "I realize that you are a ver
busy person and your time is valuable. I would be willing t
meet you whenever your schedule permits, so that I coul
have 20-30 minutes of your time."

During this time, there are processes going on both in
wardly and outwardly. Inwardly, a clearer recognition of self an
career identity is forming. Outwardly, events are unfolding t
put your puzzle pieces together.

III. Trying Out Options

As you are in career exploration, try out options before yo
take a committed step into a different career field.

Different ways to try out options include:

• *Volunteer.* Volunteer by donating a portion of your time. Ge
a taste of what it would be like in that work environment and
or career position.

This arrangement gives both you and the company time t
check each other out without a permanent commitment. I
also allows you to freely choose whether the career field is th
direction you want to continue in after having spent time in i

• *Contracting services.* Contracting services with a company is
way to try out the option of providing services while consid
ering permanent employment. Many people are hesitan
about being hired by a new company after having taken s
much time and effort to remove themselves from a dysfunc
tional organization. By contracting services the person ha
security of employment while having the independence t
consider whether permanent employment with the compan
would be a healthy choice. This employment situation is als
beneficial to someone recovering from burnout while at
tempting to make a career change.

Some people prefer contracting services over permanent employment. Examples:

Don, a computer programmer with 10 years of experience, had become exhausted and burned out dealing with "company politics." After having moved more and more of his work out of the office and into his office at home, he decided to take it a step further. He proposed to his employer that he act as a contractor instead of an employee. As a contractor, the company could use his services on special projects and when there was a work overload. During slack times the company would benefit by not carrying an employee who was not staying busy. Don could also pursue contracting with other companies in order to have a consistent work flow. Additionally, he would have the freedom to accept or reject contracts with companies he chooses, according to his desired work schedule.

Jan, a secretary, wanted to be able to have a more flexible work schedule and not be locked into a 9-to-5 job in an office building. She now contracts her services to small business owners who cannot afford a full-time employee with benefits. She is fortunate to have her benefits covered by her husband's employer. Jan finds that the variety of her work and the flexibility of her schedule has renewed the enjoyment in her work and personal life.

- *Part-time employment.* Another way to try out options is to work one or more part-time jobs in different career fields to compare their advantages and disadvantages. This option can be exciting and exhausting. You should be sure to keep balance in your life while trying this avenue of exploration.

V. Developing Skills

While you're working on resolving co-dependency issues, exploring career fields, and trying out options, start asking yourself the following questions:

What is my skill level? _____

_____

_____

Do I need more experience? _____

_____

Do I need more education? _____

_____

What kind of training would increase career mobility? _____

_____

_____

How far can I advance with the skills and education I have at this time? _____

_____

_____

Short-Term and Long-Term Goal Planning

After identifying the skills, education and training you need, it will become evident what is needed to have career mobility within a particular field. Formulate short-term and long-term plans that are practical and attainable. Assess the money, time and effort needed in pursuing any or all of these components to reach your desired career goals.

Personal Goal Planning Sheet

Short-Term Goals

	What?	How?	Steps?	Date?
Financial:				
Employment:				
Education:				

Skills building: _____

Training: _____

Long-Term Goals

	What?	How?	Steps?	Date?
Financial:	_____		1. _____	1. _____
_____			2. _____	2. _____
_____			3. _____	3. _____
Employment:	_____		1. _____	1. _____
_____			2. _____	2. _____
_____			3. _____	3. _____
Education:	_____		1. _____	1. _____
_____			2. _____	2. _____
_____			3. _____	3. _____
Skills building:	_____		1. _____	1. _____
_____			2. _____	2. _____
_____			3. _____	3. _____
Training:	_____		1. _____	1. _____
_____			2. _____	2. _____
_____			3. _____	3. _____

The Student Option

Becoming a student can be helpful to someone who needs more education or is unsure about career direction and feels trapped. Becoming a student changes the focus of your situation because you're no longer just an employee—you're a student first, and you have a job that supports you in being a student.

Sue had been working for a company for several years and knew she needed to make a change, but she was not sure how. By becoming a student, Sue no longer felt restricted by the limits of her position or the monotony of waiting for retirement. The situation flipped around! Sue as a student went to work and did her job. Her focus was on being a student instead of filling a position. By working full-time while being a student, she increased her tolerance for an uncomfortable work situation. She hoped that her life was going to change for the better. Her company supported her in being a student, and she was able to perform better in her position. She did her work and was a responsible employee, but she no longer felt trapped in the job. Eventually, Sue completed her education and was able to make a positive career transition within the organization.

V. Getting Support

Support is definitely crucial in bringing the puzzle pieces together. Support is important because it's the key ingredient. Absolutely! Support is the key ingredient in personal recovery and career recovery. Support will reveal to you who you are, increasing self-esteem. Support will encourage you to walk through the fear of all the unknowns until the pieces fit.

What's really wonderful about support is that it supplies you with patience. The majority of us are very compulsive—we want change now! We want it to happen now! Through the career-recovery process we need encouragement to be patient. We also need to have our progress validated so we are assured that we are, indeed, making progress. Being co-dependent, we don't believe it. We have to have our successes repeated to us. We need positive reinforcement of what we have accomplished so we can believe it and press on.

Judy is frustrated being a CPA. It is emotionally and physically exhausting her. She wants to change, but to give up the CPA identity is too frightening for her. Judy has been learning that having supportive persons who believe in her ability to find a fulfilling career is crucial for her transition. Judy has been able to edge out and explore career options while being supported by people who believe in her. In time, belief in herself will become her reality by walking through the fear, by learning the skill, by making it her own. That's when the belief and behavior will be hers. By making it her own and living it, there is a foundation of self-confidence to build on.

Support helps us to pursue. Support helps us to be persistent. Support helps us maintain commitment to self. Part of that is trusting inside and outside timing. During this time, tell your Higher Power, "Hey, look, I'm doing my part. You've got to do your part. I'm keeping up my side of the bargain. You've got to keep up your side of the bargain." There is an inward timing that is attained by personal-recovery work. There is an outward timing of unfolding life events, such as meeting the right person or opening the right door so that events can come together. Nothing is worse for compulsive people than the torture of limbo. It is like having a car in neutral while you gun the engine. Trust your inward timing. Trust your Higher Power for the outside timing. As the inward timing unfolds, we find our answers about our lives and our careers. Outward answers do take place, and the puzzle comes together.

Chapter 3

The Lost Self at Work

Co-dependency in a person's career is experienced each day in co-dependent employee behavior. Be assured that co-dependent employees are doing their best to make their positions work for them. Co-dependent employees have the best intentions. They believe their co-dependent approach is based on what it takes to be a "good employee." As one of my clients stated, "I have found out that what I thought were my strongest attributes as a valuable employee are co-dependent." In this chapter we will examine how co-dependency is detrimental to the employee as well as the organization.

Let's look at how co-dependency is acted out in the workplace in dysfunctional work relationships. These beliefs and behaviors are the foundation on which dysfunctional organizations continue to operate.

Here is a list of co-dependent employee beliefs. Circle each statement *True* or *False* as it applies to you in your workplace.

1. I am aware of what supervisors, co-workers and clients feel and want, rather than what I feel and want.

TRUE   FALSE

2. My attention is focused on pleasing my supervisors
   co-workers or clients and receiving their approval.

   TRUE   FALSE

3. Fear of rejection determines what I say and do at work.

   TRUE   FALSE

4. Fear of anger from my supervisors, co-workers or client
   determines what I say and do in the workplace.

   TRUE   FALSE

5. I use giving as a way of feeling safe in work relationships.

   TRUE   FALSE

6. I value the opinion of my supervisors or co-workers and the
   way they perform work more than my own.

   TRUE   FALSE

7. Staff struggles at work affect my peace of mind.

   TRUE   FALSE

8. My self-esteem and mental attention is focused on solving
   problems my supervisors, co-workers or clients may have.

   TRUE   FALSE

9. My attention is focused on protecting my supervisor's o
   co-worker's employment position.

   TRUE   FALSE

10. My attention is focused on manipulating my supervisors
    co-workers or clients to "do it my way" in the workplace.

    TRUE   FALSE

Now, for every *True* you circled, you have identified *a majo
belief and behavior of a co-dependent employee.*

Because of these beliefs and behaviors, the co-dependen
dynamic reinforces the common problems that co-dependen
employees experience in the workplace. This leads to continua

ustration and anxiety in their career and work performance.
These mutual co-dependent issues thwart the efforts of the
erson to achieve personal and professional satisfaction.

COMMON PROBLEMS OF CO-DEPENDENT EMPLOYEES

1. *Co-dependent employees have difficulty accurately identifying and expressing their feelings.* Co-dependent people have been taught not to feel or express feelings. Because of this, they feel numb or confused when disruptive situations take place. Co-dependent employees are quite fearful of the anger they feel and carry with them. They have done a pretty good job of suppressing this anger and are terrified of letting go of it.

   Co-dependent employees have not been taught the skills they need to deal with and express their feelings appropriately. Therefore, in the workplace they do not accurately identify feelings. When co-dependent employees do identify a feeling, they are not able to express the feeling appropriately.

2. *Co-dependent employees have difficulty in forming trusting relationships with supervisors and/or co-workers.* Because the co-dependent employees were unable to trust the people who were supposed to support them emotionally during childhood, in adulthood co-dependents gravitate toward untrustworthy people. They endure a history in which others take advantage of them and emotionally hurt them, reinforcing their belief that they cannot trust anyone.

3. *Co-dependent employees have an unrealistic expectation of perfectionism for themselves and others.* In a dysfunctional system, perfectionism is the goal a co-dependent employee strives to reach. This goal can never be attained, and the employee is emotionally "beat up" by not attaining this perfection. No matter how good, how successful, or how outstanding the co-dependent employee may be, she always feels less,

because her yardstick of perfection is never attained, again being reinforced by dysfunctional systems that pressure the co-dependent employee to attain perfection.

4. *Co-dependent employees have a rigid view of life and experience difficulty in adjusting to change.* They are rigid because of the strict rules they follow that formulate the beliefs and behaviors of a dysfunctional system. This strict view of life encourages the co-dependent employee to hold on to the black-and-white rules of the organization, restricting him from having a broader view of options and choices in the career and work environment.

Rigidity and routine gives the co-dependent employee a false sense of security. He believes he has control of his world and is safe because of this rigid view. It also assists him in repeating and maintaining dysfunctional practices because of his fear of change, even though it would be for the better. Change makes him extremely fearful, and he feels out of control. Difficulty in adjusting to change reinforces the idea that the employee does not have the true conviction of who he is. He is not confident that he has or can make a choice.

5. *Co-dependent employees feel overly responsible for the behavior and feeling of other staff members in the work environment.* Feeling overly responsible for an inadequate supervisor or co-worker can throw a co-dependent employee into overextending himself in order to compensate for the supervisor's or co-worker's irresponsibility.

Co-dependent employees often take on more responsibilities than are required by their job description. They extend themselves emotionally and physically beyond what is ever healthy. Many co-dependent employees work themselves into the stress of physical and mental overload, which leads to burnout and sometimes to suicide. Again, co-dependent employees feel overly responsible for others. They are out of touch with the need to be responsible for themselves.

6. *Co-dependent employees need constant approval in order to feel good about themselves.* The co-dependent employee constantly strives for approval from others to feel good about himself. Since co-dependent employees are not strong in self-image, they do not have internal reserves of self-esteem and constantly run on empty. They focus all their time and energy in gaining others' approval.

Co-dependent employees set themselves up for total emotional and physical deprivation in order to gain this approval. They hand all their power over to others. They rely on the approval or rejection of others to define their lives.

7. *Co-dependent employees have difficulty in making decisions.* The co-dependent employee seeking constant approval from others is unqualified to make decisions. Co-dependent employees make decisions according to what the other staff members want. It's very difficult for co-dependent employees to make a decision if they don't know what their supervisor or co-worker wants. To gain approval, they will try to guess which decision will be pleasing to a supervisor or co-worker.

Left to themselves, co-dependent employees have extreme anxiety making decisions they are responsible for. Making decisions that will be approved by others is a way to protect themselves and diminish responsibility for the decision.

8. *Co-dependent employees avoid conflict and anger at all costs.* Co-dependent employees avoid conflict and are fearful of anger from others because of the inappropriate expression of anger or rage that occurred in their childhood. Even if the anger or rage was not openly expressed, it significantly affects the employee's ability to cope with conflict.

Co-dependent employees fear they might say or do something that will make their supervisors or co-workers angry. They are fearful that they will be fired or rejected. This fear of rejection keeps the co-dependent employee from causing any conflict even when the ultimate cost is his emotional and physical health.

9. *Co-dependent employees feel powerless and helpless to make any change.* Co-dependent employees give all their power to another person, avoid conflict and "perform" in order to achieve approval. They do not express their views or how they see things in the work environment.

It is impossible for co-dependent employees' needs to be met in the workplace under these conditions. They feel powerless to make change in the work environment and resign themselves to that fact.

Because of their nonassertive behavior and their diligence in giving power away to others, they become despondent and frustrated about change in their environment or career. They are locked into the co-dependent view of life. They cannot integrate their personal and professional image. They do not have the strength or conviction to fight for their personal and professional needs.

10. *Co-dependent employees have low self-image.* They continually seek the approval of others in order to experience some degree of self-acceptance. Co-dependent employees continue the behaviors that constantly reinforce the belief that they are "less than." This vicious cycle reinforces itself, and co-dependent employees believe this as truth.

Co-dependent employees begin to realize that, much to their surprise, these co-dependent behaviors do not work for them, yet they doggedly hold on to the distorted rules that keep co-dependency active. One rule that keeps co-dependent employee beliefs intact is: Don't communicate openly or honestly with co-workers and supervisors. Another rule directs employees to never show human frailties such as weakness, fear, anger, exhaustion, confusion or disappointment.

RULES THAT KEEP EMPLOYEES STUCK IN CO-DEPENDENT BEHAVIOR

1. The co-dependent employee maintains the unrealistic expectation that he or she will always be a good employee, always be a strong person, always be a perfect employee and always maintain a pleasant disposition.

2. The co-dependent employee is always a "team player."

3. The co-dependent employee does not talk about corporate or personnel problems.

4. The co-dependent employee does not express true feelings to supervisors or co-workers.

5. The co-dependent employee communicates by using a messenger between two primary people who need to talk directly to each other (triangulation).

6. The co-dependent employee expects others to "Do as I say, not as I do."

7. It is not OK for the co-dependent employee to be playful or lighthearted.

8. The co-dependent employee maintains control at all costs, even when it means jeopardizing his or her physical and emotional health.

These rules all serve to protect and isolate co-dependent employees from becoming empowered persons. Therefore they don't know who they are or what they want, and they are unable to express that in the work environment.

RESULTS OF CO-DEPENDENT EMPLOYEE BEHAVIOR

1. Loss of true identity as a person and professional.

2. Professional identity does not match the true self.

3. Limited in professional and personal growth.

4. Low self-esteem is continually reinforced.

5. Does not receive, or voids recognition of a job well done.

6. Sets up the dynamics to be victimized by co-workers, clients and supervisors.

7. Feels frustrated and helpless to improve the work situation.

8. Decisions are made according to fears and need for control in the workplace.

9. Tends to mistreat others to get ahead in his/her career.

10. Personal and professional potential is not fully experienced.

The results of these beliefs and the continuing problems take a devastating toll over time. This distorted way of life becomes the reality for the co-dependent employee.

While working with hundreds of co-dependent employees on the work site and in career transition, I have discovered five basic adult employee roles. There is a correlation between the childhood roles co-dependent employees are groomed in and the extended roles they act out in the workplace.

GROWING UP CO-DEPENDENT FROM CHILDHOOD TO THE WORKPLACE

Childhood Roles	*Adult Employee Roles*
Miniparent	Wonderful Worker
Troublemaker	Angry Avenger
Shadow	Chameleon
Tension Breaker	Joker
Talking Head*	

*Adapted as a combination of adult roles: usually Wonderful Worker and Chameleon.

The Different Faces of Co-dependent Employees

1. *The Wonderful Worker.* This employee always has a smile on her face. She will do everything in her power to keep her

employer and co-workers happy at the cost of personal health and sanity. The wonderful worker tends to be a nurturing parent to co-workers.

2. *The Angry Avenger.* The Angry Avenger is the employee who is always angry and always carries a chip on his shoulder. This person usually has a long history of anger. It's a wonderful defense mechanism to keep people away from him. It is also a great way for him to intimidate others and get his way.

3. *The Chameleon.* This employee changes into whatever the situation demands. She will use all of her energy to assess a particular situation and conform to that predicament. The co-dependent employee will blend in and not share her own views or give her own opinion (she doesn't usually know what it is anyway). What she will repeat is the opinion and views of those that she is reflecting.

4. *The Joker.* The Joker is quite funny, has wonderful jokes, and is entertaining when he isn't extremely depressed. The joker treats life as a joke. There are no serious issues. Everything's funny. He uses his humor to break up tension in the work environment or relieve upset between co-workers. The sad situation is that the joker believes himself to be the joke. It's difficult to deal openly and honestly with this employee because the joker hides behind his jokes.

5. *The Talking Head.* The Talking Head lives from the neck up and has a computerized printout of life. Emotions are not to be felt or dealt with. Feelings don't compute. This person is usually an accountant, architect, lawyer, engineer, etc. Life is viewed, like Mr. Spock from the television series *Star Trek*, as only being dealt with logically. Emotions are overwhelming and produce a sense of being out of control. A Talking Head would rather bypass emotions and have a computerized printout on how to live life.

ROLES THAT I PLAY

What Role Did I Play Growing Up?

Miniparent

Troublemaker

Shadow

Tension Breaker

Combination of Roles

What Role Do I Play At Work?

Wonderful Worker

Angry Avenger

Chameleon

Joker

Talking Head

Combination of Roles

1. Are they the same or different? _____

_____

_____

2. What is the advantage of the role? _____

_____

_____

3. What is the disadvantage of the role? _____

_____

_____

4. What roles do I observe in the workplace? _____

_____

_____

THE COUNTERDEPENDENT CONNECTION

Now that I have clarified what co-dependency is, it is time to look at the other side of a dysfunctional work relationship, counterdependency. A co-dependent's approach to a work relationship is giving himself away to feel safe. The other side of this partnership usually includes a counterdependent person. The counterdependent person approaches the work relationship by taking over control to feel safe in the partnership.

Materials developed by Claudia Black and Terry Gorski, as well as Claudia's workshops on "Recovery in Relationships," mention information about the co-dependent/counterdependent relationship between men and women in their personal lives. This same dynamic is true in work relationships between clients, co-workers, supervisors, managers, executives, partners and owners. Over the last 30 years, alcohol/drug abuse has been brought out of the closet and exposed for the long-term damaging effects on the addicted person, his family and job. In like manner there are long-term damaging effects of a counterdependent employee on himself, fellow employees and the work environment. A counterdependent employee abuses power, especially power over people. Until now counterdependent employees have been viewed as "take charge" people, highly competitive, outspoken, "go-getters," aggressive, ambitious, hardliners, dedicated, steadfast, high achievers . . . and the list goes on. When these attributes are distorted by the abuse of power and control, the counterdependent person can become a leading source of dysfunction in the workplace.

We need employees to take the lead and be committed to bottom-line results, but not at the expense of depleting staff members emotionally and physically, causing dysfunction in the work relationships.

Power and control are the primary motivators of counterdependent employees. Their belief system reinforces this focus and becomes quite evident in their dealing with fellow employees. The following list helps identify this belief system:

COUNTERDEPENDENT EMPLOYEE BELIEFS

1. Counterdependent employees are aware of what they want and do not take into consideration the feelings or needs of others.

2. Counterdependent employees focus their attention on pleasing themselves, even at the expense of other employees.

3. Fearing loss of control or loss of power determines what counterdependent employees say or do.

4. Counterdependent employees use anger to control, intimidate and make others do what they want.

5. Counterdependent employees "take over" in situations to feel safe in work relationships.

6. Counterdependent employees see only their side of any situation.

7. Counterdependent employees don't want to be bothered by life issues and feelings of other staff members.

8. Counterdependent employees focus their attention on solving problems their way, no matter how others are affected.

9. Counterdependent employees focus their attention on protecting their position and power, whether or not it disrupts the work environment or is costly to other employees.

10. Counterdependent employees focus their attention on making others do things their way.

CO-DEPENDENT/ COUNTERDEPENDENT WORK RELATIONSHIPS

Co-dependent employees have basic low self-esteem due to chronic loss of self throughout their lives. In the workplace co-dependents act on this insecurity by being other-centered. They believe that as long as they can meet the needs of others, their needs will automatically be met. Being overly dependent on others, they look to others for acceptance and validation. Because of these beliefs, co-dependent employees do not have defined boundaries that would protect them from being exploited by others in the workplace.

Because of this dynamic, co-dependent employees are continually finding themselves in dysfunctional work relationships with counterdependent co-workers, supervisors, managers and business partners.

What co-dependent and counterdependent employees have in common is fear. They both are centered in insecurity and low self-esteem. The co-dependent employee protects himself by giving his attention to others in an effort to gain security through acceptance from others. They believe that if they conform to what the other person wants, everything will just be fine. The more a co-dependent employee's fear of rejection escalates, the more he overextends himself to others.

The opposite is true of counterdependent employees. Their insecurity and low self-esteem motivates them to protect themselves by maintaining power and control over others. Through seclusion and self-involvement, they maintain a fortress of protection. They believe that they can rely only on themselves. They do not have respect for fallible human beings who make mistakes. Counterdependents set unrealistically high goals for themselves and expect everyone else to live up to them. Positions of power and control are the points of advantage counterdependent employees intend on keeping over their own life and everybody else's.

Counterdependent employees' fears increase if co-dependent employees attempt to become independent of their control, even in small issues. Their reaction to this independence is to assert more control, using anger, intimidation, hurt, guilt and threats of job termination or demotions. Counterdependent employees feel they are entitled to whatever is the co-dependent's area—desk, office, files or belongings. Whatever they need or want should be theirs. If that means going through another employee's desk, removing papers from the files, or helping themselves to supplies without asking, their attitude is "So what?" They are "entitled" to whatever they feel they need or want. Counterdependent employees' boundaries are barriers that protect them and at the same time overextend into other employees' domain without regard or respect for the rights of other employees. Treating others without the same respect that they expect is the hallmark of counterdependent employees. If anyone would treat them in like manner there would be "hell to pay."

Due to these control issues, basic disrespect for co-dependents and preoccupation with their own needs, counterdependent employees can be the *leading cause of dysfunction in a department or organization*.

This dysfunctional work relationship is acted out in a variety of scenarios. Ultimately it reduces co-dependent employees to emotionally and physically drained individuals who feel frustrated and trapped in hopeless predicaments. Their self-esteem is so bruised and battered that they don't believe they could find employment anywhere else. Fear of change is overwhelming, and they are resigned to be sentenced to "doing their time" in emotional lockup. Counterdependent employees are baffled by the reactions or resentments of the co-dependent employees who have been pressed beyond their emotional and physical limits. They believe that they have done their job maintaining discipline in order to get the job done. They view co-dependent employees not as people but as producers. They believe that "personal issues are to be left at the door and picked up on the way out." Their work motto is "My way or the highway."

Working in a dysfunctional work relationship with counter-dependents will cause the co-dependents to constantly "walk on eggshells" in an attempt to maintain the status quo of perfection that can never be attained.

I must point out that it is possible at times for individuals to demonstrate either co-dependent or counterdependent traits. When an occasion arises that would put the co-dependent person in a power role, this sometimes happens. It is also possible for a person to show stronger co-dependent or counter-dependent traits in either the home or work environment. The important issue here is that both the co-dependent's and counterdependent's traits rob a person of fulfillment and satisfaction in work relationships. Both lose in the struggle to protect their fragile, low self-esteem.

The Cycle of Co-dependent Hope

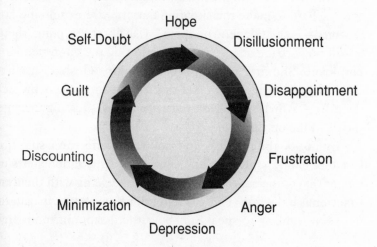

Co-dependent employees constantly are caught in dysfunctional work relationships with counterdependent co-workers and supervisors.

The pattern of the Cycle of Co-dependent Hope starts with hope—hope that is based on a fantasy conversation in the co-dependent employee's mind without being grounded in a verbal exchange with the other employee involved. The co-dependent employee does not clarify the guideline expectations and commitment to the project beforehand. The fantasy conversation is one of hopefulness that the other person will invest as much time, money, energy, etc., into any given project as the co-dependent herself is investing. The co-dependent person may be aware that this other person has never followed through in previous projects, nor given her credit, supported her efforts or held up the responsibility she committed to. Nevertheless, fantasy hope is the foundation of this cycle.

In a short time the co-dependent employee realizes things are not going as "hoped for." She has held on to an illusion that does not match the reality. Soon she becomes disillusioned. It becomes evident that the co-dependent employee is carrying the load again. Disillusionment quickly advances into disappointment. "I thought it would be different this time." "I tried so hard to make the situation better." "They told me not to worry—I could depend on them." Usually at this point, there is still no verbal exchange or discussion by the co-dependent employee. She may put out big hints like, "Gosh, I sure am tired of putting in 12 hours a day, trying to get this project done!" or "Wow! Are you as tired as I am from pressing to make the deadline on this project?!"

By not dealing openly and pointedly with the issue, the Cycle of Co-dependent Hope continues. Frustration starts to mount due to the continued avoidance of dealing with the dysfunctional behavior. The co-dependent employee is caught between wanting to speak up about the disappointment and feeling too fearful or unsure of how to resolve the issue. If the co-dependent person does attempt to speak up, the effort usually proves unsuccessful due to inability to clearly define expectations and hold others accountable.

Anger erupts inwardly if not outwardly. This anger may be directed inappropriately or at persons not related to the real issue.

Many co-dependent employees immediately suppress anger and shift into depression. Depression is anger turned inward, and if the anger is not dealt with appropriately and according to the situation, the person turns the anger on herself. Depression magnifies the feeling of helplessness and the feeling of no way out.

Minimization begins after a time in depression and numerous hours of replaying the whole saga of events leading up to this point. Minimizing shrinks events down to manageable size for the co-dependent, who is not strong enough in self-image to deal with the reality of the situation. The co-dependent employee minimizes the events by convincing herself that the situation "wasn't that big of a deal." After the situation is shrunken down to size, the next step is to discount the whole event. "The deadline was met. The project is over. I don't know why I made such a big deal about it anyway."

Now the co-dependent is ready to shift into guilt for thinking such ugly thoughts, getting angry or being so insensitive. The list goes on and on. Guilt assists co-dependents in discrediting themselves and believing they are all wrong.

The outcome of the Cycle of Co-dependent Hope is crippled self-esteem and overwhelming self-doubt. Co-dependents are emotionally, physically and spiritually depleted from this process. Their sense of what is real or imagined is distorted to the point that they do not know what to think. "Was I asking too much?" "Maybe they really did the best job they could." "She did say she was tired from working so hard." "But I did do double the work and handled my regular job duties." "Well, I probably should be more understanding, since her dog was pregnant and was ready to deliver at any time." "I just need to work harder and not spend so much time complaining." "It will be better next time!" The stage is set, and the co-dependent is ready to enter again into the "Fantasy Hope Zone." Another project will come up, fantasy hope will lull the co-dependent person into a false sense of security, hints will be dropped and the Cycle of Co-dependent Hope will start all over again.

The Counterdependent Stance

The counterdependent's stance during the Cycle of Co-dependent Hope is to dig in and hold on to power and control. The message, "Do it my way: don't speak up or challenge me," is clear and constant. The co-dependent is going through emotional gymnastics during the 10 phases of this cycle, while the counterdependent stance stays constant.

While the co-dependent tries to break the Cycle of Co-dependent Hope, the counterdependent reacts by using whatever he can to prevent the co-dependent's success. Threats, anger, outbursts, silence, pouting, blaming, intimidation, hurt, tears and/or rage are used by the counterdependent employee in an effort to keep the co-dependent on the cycle course.

RESOLUTION AND CHANGE

Usually a situation has to become quite serious before a co-dependent employee decides to resolve dysfunctional behaviors. Change happens when the pain becomes too great to endure the situation any longer. The old way of behavior leads to exhaustion by continuing the same patterns that do not attain the desired goals.

When the employee decides to face the issues that promote dysfunction, it is time to implement change. This Healthy Change Process (Chapter 5) must coincide with a step-by-step plan to resolve the dysfunctional performance and implement a healthy way to function.

It is important to note that the Healthy Change Process takes time in order to implement healthier beliefs and behaviors. Allow adequate time for this process in order to ensure stability. In this way the employee will not be overwhelmed with too much change at one time.

Support is one of the most important ingredients during this time. It takes positive support to change the dysfunctional system and co-dependent beliefs, to gain the skills to have a healthy work environment and to experience interdependence (Chapter 4) among employees.

THE INGREDIENTS OF SELF-ESTEEM

During the process of resolving these co-dependency issues, developing self-esteem is essential. The ingredients for developing healthy self-esteem are as follows:

1. Respect from others and yourself.

2. Acceptance from others and yourself.

3. Love from others and yourself.

4. Exercising power over your own life.

5. Setting goals and attaining them.

6. Living your life according to your values and beliefs.

7. Taking responsibility for your actions, both positive and negative.

The skills that fortify self-esteem and enhance self-image need to be learned and exercised throughout the Healthy Change Process. In this way the skills will become part of the employee's daily life.

These skills will only be truly effective by learning a new way of healthy living.

Remember that change often affects those supervisors, co-workers or clients around you. Personal change may make others uncomfortable, hurt, fearful, angry and resentful. It's important to be considerate of others without sacrificing personal needs. Remember, it is possible to fulfill personal and professional needs without continuing co-dependent behaviors.

Take time to celebrate the successes of change, no matter how small. Again, support is an important component, since co-dependent employees usually don't pay attention to their own successes. It is important to share your successes with others and have others repeat your successes back to you.

LIVING IN THE GRAY

Co-dependent employees live their lives in a black-and-white world of good/bad and right/wrong. When resolving co-dependency issues, it is important to understand that balance and consistency are the goals for living a healthy life.

Living in the gray means that the employee should not take a completely opposite approach to life in order to compensate for being co-dependent. For example, I have seen co-dependent people who had spent most of their lives bending over backwards to assist and please others. When they realize they are co-dependent, they decide never to do another kind thing for anyone. The black-and-white world of the co-dependent employee does not work in the recovery process.

Living in the gray means being attentive to the needs of self and others in a balanced way. First, one should take care of personal needs, and then extend the appropriate balance of emotional, spiritual and physical abilities to others accordingly.

In a work environment where a co-dependent employee has been doing the work of another employee, it is important for the co-dependent to be responsible for only his own job requirements while maintaining the team approach that involves project deadlines and other situations that occur within a work environment. Again, living in the gray is a tenuous position. Practice and time will help strengthen the employee's ability to stay balanced and consistent within his job duties.

One of the toughest times for co-dependents to live in the gray is when they are discerning clear job responsibilities. During these times they need to focus on their own limits and detach from the other person's responsibilities. Carefully separate and delineate the two. Supervisory clarification is crucial to help employees maintain balance and to avoid triggering co-dependent behavior that might result in relapse into dysfunction. Living in the gray challenges one to be true to self and others in a balanced, consistent way.

WHAT DOES HEALTHY BEHAVIOR LOOK LIKE?

1. The healthy employee is responsible for his/her job duties and does not take on another employee's responsibilities.
2. The healthy employee gives honest feedback and input into staff meetings, discussions, procedures, etc.
3. The healthy employee is able to clearly state what is and is not possible for him/her to complete in order to make a deadline.
4. The healthy employee speaks up clearly and firmly when faced with a personal injustice.
5. The healthy employee is supportive of co-worker accomplishments.
6. The healthy employee works to the best of his/her ability and deals with mistakes appropriately.
7. The healthy employee asks for increased responsibilities and duties when he/she feels ready to fulfill those responsibilities.

Healthy behavior occurs when employees recognize what is possible and make changes within the work environment that will promote a healthier environment. They also recognize what is not possible and make the best decision according to the situation.

Healthy behavior is reflected by employees who express their true identity and come into their full professional potential. These employees value the talents of their co-workers and practice collaboration instead of control.

WHAT DOES HEALTHY BEHAVIOR FEEL LIKE?

Healthy behavior feels uncomfortable at times because the individual has become accustomed to crisis, confusion and frustration. It takes practice to become comfortable with balance in one's life. Healthy behavior can also be uncomfortable when it is not accepted by loved ones, co-workers and supervisors who have become accustomed to the employee's co-dependency. It has been to their advantage to have the employee's co-dependency continue.

Healthy behavior restores mental, spiritual and physical energy. Experiencing the effects of healthier behaviors increases a self-supportive approach to life.

ENVIRONMENTS THAT ARE TOXIC

Toxic organizations are indeed dysfunctional, but there are dysfunctional organizations that are not toxic. The point is that dysfunction can be worked with and improved to some degree by all people involved. The core of the dysfunctional organization is the intention to control. *The toxic organization's core focus is to control and emotionally possess employees by being the total source of validation, security and identity to the employee. Toxic organizations will not tolerate employees resolving their own co-dependency issues.*

In a toxic work environment, invalidation of an employee's contribution, opinion and self-image is a continuing message. Employees can get caught trying to fight the invalidation of their work and self-esteem. What fortifies this invalidation is that the employees rarely if ever receive compliments or accolades for work well done, money saved by the company or new clients brought on board by their efforts.

A prevalent sign of a toxic work environment is employees walking on eggshells and whispering to each other in corners to make "allies." The hope is that these allies will secure them against the anger and wrath of the unpredictable toxic manager or co-worker. This unpredictability and anger can be acted out nonverbally as well as verbally and physically.

Employees band together in an effort to survive the emotional abuse in the workplace. They encourage each other during this continuing drama. The toxicity continues to deplete the employees emotionally, spiritually and physically. Toxic work environments demean employees over time, making them feel unworthy and unable to find other work. It depletes the positive advances they have made resolving their co-dependency issues. In this weakened condition, with the negative assessment of their abilities and skills, the employees are gripped with debilitating fear. They start to question whether they should even consider looking for other employment. Hopelessness becomes emotionally crippling.

The fear of change keeps them in the cycle of dysfunction, and low self-image perpetuates their continued emotional abuse in the toxic environment. If this emotional abuse continues, the employees will sabotage whatever accomplishments they have gained in developing themselves.

In a toxic work environment, an employee is not be able to exercise creativity because all time and attention is drained by the toxic environment. Work becomes a survival situation in which the employee's energy is depleted. In time this will lead to stress, burnout and health problems.

THE "BROKEN PICKER" SYNDROME

Resolving co-dependency issues and establishing a more healthy lifestyle is the basis for fixing your "picker" (your capacity to choose). The "Broken Picker" Syndrome occurs when people continue to select the wrong careers and work environments. Their "pickers" are broken because their low self-image invalidates their abilities and strengths. It is this invalidation of self that has been perpetuated throughout their lives.

A "broken picker" can cause us to select and bring toxic people into our lives. By developing self-esteem and coming into our true self, our picker will automatically recover. The more healthy we become, the more healthy our pickers become.

When employees have healthy pickers, they choose healthy friends, healthy relationships and a healthy work environments. Their career identities become an expression of their true selves.

HEALTHY WORK ENVIRONMENTS

When an individual is in a healthy work environment, it will nurture him or her emotionally, physically and spiritually. A healthy work environment promotes creativity, development of professional skills, and expression of true self and career identity.

A healthy work environment is crucial for employees to come into the full expression of who they are personally and professionally. When employees are in healthy work environments, they do not have to expend their energy to guard and protect themselves. They are free to breathe easily and be in touch with their true selves instead of numbing themselves for survival. In the expression of true self, creativity is evident and realized through career identity.

POSITION, POWER AND POSSIBILITIES

When employees are dealing with resolving their co-dependency issues and establishing new beliefs and behaviors, it is important to evaluate the comfort zone within the work situation.

Many employees would like to be able to implement healthy change without jeopardizing their current positions. Others who are considering a career move would like to maintain a sense of calm and balance in the workplace while investigating other career options. And there are those of us who want to revolutionize the entire organization by confronting all dysfunction.

No matter what the intention, it is important to realize the impact of one's position, how much power one has or doesn't have, as well as the possibilities that exist within a particular situation.

Usually when employees come to the point of realizing that change has to occur, it is because they can no longer continue with the way things are. They also believe everyone else needs to change to make it work.

Even though it would be great for everyone to break the cycle of dysfunction, usually the work environment limits our impact.

For example, if an employee holds a secretarial position, her power will be limited and her possibilities will be proportioned accordingly. She will be able to increase her comfort zone by limiting her co-dependent behavior and implementing a certain degree of healthy behavior.

On the other hand, if her position is manager of a department, she will have more power to implement guidelines throughout the department to minimize dysfunction and limit co-dependent/counterdependent behavior. An employee's awareness of her position, power and possibilities for change will help her realize to what degree she will be able to comfortably function within a dysfunctional situation.

It will also help employees to have a clearer view of the time line they will need to use during a career-transition period.

Position, Power and Possibilities Worksheet

Position

What position do I hold?

How long have I held this position?

What are the co-dependent impacts on self/others?

What are the counterdependent impacts on self/others?

Power

How much power do I have in my position to implement healthy change?

Can I exercise this power in my position? Why? Why not?

Do I have support of those in power? Why? Why not?

• Possibilities

What is the possible outcome of discontinuing my co-dependent behavior in the workplace?

Positive Outcomes

1. _____
2. _____
3. _____
4. _____

Negative Outcomes

1. _____
2. _____
3. _____
4. _____

Comfort Zone in the Workplace/Career

On a scale of 1 (least) to 10 (best), where is my comfort-zone score in the workplace? _____

On a scale of 1 (least) to 10 (best), where is my comfort-zone score in my career? _____

What do I need to increase my comfort zone in the workplace?

_____

What do I need to increase my comfort zone in my career?

_____

Time Line

How long can I stay in this workplace under these conditions?

_____

How long can I stay in my career under these conditions?

_____

According to my time line, what are three things I can do to assist in improving the workplace conditions?

1. _____ Date to be done _____

2. _____ Date to be done _____

3. _____ Date to be done _____

According to my time line, what are three things I can do to assist in my career transition?

1. _____ Date to be done _____

2. _____ Date to be done _____

3. _____ Date to be done _____

Chapter 4

Team versus Terrorism

Stephen P. Robbins, in his book, *Organizational Behavior: Concepts, Controversies, and Applications*, defines an organization as "the planned coordination of the activities of two or more people in order to achieve some common and explicit goal through division of labor and a hierarchy of authority." The intent of an organization is to have a system that operates properly to produce a product, generate a profit, handle employees and meet customer demands.

Even though the intent of the organization is admirable, if the belief system and behavioral practices are dysfunctional, the reality will be as follows:

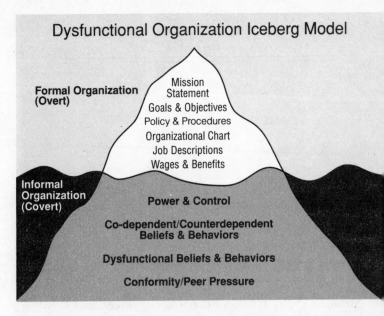

Using the Dysfunctional Organization Iceberg Model, note that the top (exposed) part of the organization may appear to have excellent standards, procedures and product success, but it is the bottom or hidden part that is the true test of the health or dysfunction of an organization.

The top part of the iceberg consists of the formal organization (overt portion). This formal part includes the organization's mission statement, policies, procedures, organizational chart and job descriptions. Goals and objectives describe the direction the organization is headed and what it plans to achieve.

On the surface, everything may look professional to the outside observer. Just as an iceberg can conceal the danger beneath the water line, so can a dysfunctional organization give the illusion that there is nothing wrong with this picture. If we don't look deeper, we will be lulled into a false sense of security believing everything is "just fine."

The bottom part of the iceberg is the informal organization, the real life and the heartbeat of the organization. In a dysfunctional organization the informal organization is composed of power and control, co-dependent/counterdependent beliefs and behaviors, dysfunctional beliefs and behaviors, and conformity and peer pressure.

Most employees in a dysfunctional organization are not fully aware of the toxicity and crises in which they function until the effect becomes extremely exhausting. Because of dysfunctional backgrounds, co-dependent employees have been groomed to believe dysfunction is "normal."

While consulting to a federal agency, I interviewed 15 employees who averaged more than 10 years of service.

Every one of them reported extreme emotional exhaustion and physical ailments due to stress. I explained to them the dysfunctional issues that contributed to the level of stress and burnout they were experiencing. Because they were so used to working in such dysfunction, it was difficult for them to believe that there was a healthier way to manage people and perform their jobs. They were like the survivors on the Titanic wondering what had happened after they crashed into the unknown dangers that lay waiting beneath the water line.

Benefits, perks, a good wage, loyalty to co-workers/clients and job security can numb employees to the emotional and physical impact of working in a dysfunctional organization.

Dysfunctional organizations include the following components that constitute dysfunction. These components are necessary for the work environment to maintain and encourage co-dependent/counterdependent work relationships. On the other hand, co-dependent/counterdependent work relationships make a dysfunctional organization function. Both the dysfunctional environment and co-dependent/counterdependent employee culture keep the dysfunctional "ball" rolling.

COMPONENTS OF A DYSFUNCTIONAL ORGANIZATION

1. Conformity
2. Denial
3. Crisis and Confusion
4. Self-Centeredness
5. Dishonesty
6. Perfectionism
7. Control
8. The "Carrot Promise"
9. Invalidation of Viewpoints
10. Dualism: Black-and-White Rules
11. Branding: Disloyal/Not a Team Player

Conformity

The basic issue with a dysfunctional organization is that everyone is pressed to conform to the informal dysfunctional "standard," which sets the stage for dysfunction because the employee is expected to take on the identity of the company culture. The emphasis is on what straightjacket the company expects the employee to wear in order to be "part of the team." Individuality is restricted and rejected. Conformity is the requirement for one to receive approval in a dysfunctional organization.

Denial

Denial of problems can take many forms, from allowing an employee to continue abusing alcohol or drugs to constantly sinking time and money into a project (or department) that is not productive and ignoring staff unrest.

Denial means that an organization is determined to avoid facing the real problem, especially if the real problem is a counterdependent employee in a powerful position within the company—or that a counterdependent influences a decision-making person within the organization. By not dealing with the dysfunction of the counterdependent employee as a problem, he is free to continue his "reign of terror." Intimidating and controlling everything and everybody causes constant upheaval and distress among staff. The atmosphere is charged by his presence and negative attitude.

Usually a dysfunctional organization is willing to deal with the formal issues of a problem—the cosmetic approach. It is the informal segment of the organization where the resistance to face the real problem occurs. Many times this resistance and denial at the informal level occurs because the organization does not respond to the problem and the impact of the problem. Organizations are so used to living with the problem that it has been accepted as a part of life within the organization.

Everyone is expected to live with the problem. "That's just how it is!"

Crisis and Confusion

Crisis and confusion keep denial intact. Constant crisis and confusion cause employees to believe the crisis is the serious problem. Everything becomes a crisis except the real issue. Crisis keeps the focus off the real issue. For example, an emergency memo states that everyone is to have "only one lead pencil sharpened on his desk at all times." Employees are too busy ensuring that they have one sharpened lead pencil on their desk at all times to look beyond the crisis and deal with the true problem in the organization. Crisis and confusion keep employees off balance. They lose a clear perspective and the power to make positive change in dealing with the real problem.

When a new employee naively points out that the company has a problem, management will redirect the employee's attention off the problem and onto an inconsequential matter. He will be asked, "Do you have a sharpened lead pencil on your desk?" Caught in crisis and confusion, the employee runs to get a pencil and drops the topic of the problem. Crisis and confusion continue. Soon the new employee ignores the real problem and focuses on the lead pencil, like everyone else.

At times an organization will cause crisis and confusion because the tension of not dealing with the real problem is so high. Often the focus will be turned on the individual who is pointing out the real problem. He will be seen as the real problem and as a troublemaker affecting the organization's productivity. "If he weren't such a troublemaker, everything would be all right!"

Troublemakers are usually speaking the truth in some way, so the truth becomes the problem. The organization then focuses on keeping employees from speaking the truth. Pressure increases. Soon the organization will have everyone working overtime and running in several directions at once. Employees will focus on protecting their positions. Crisis and confusion are heightened, affecting productivity, job satisfaction and morale, and increasing stress and burnout. The employees are then much too exhausted and depleted to do anything except survive the constant upheaval of crisis and confusion.

Self-Centeredness

As I went into one company I saw a sign on the wall that said, "My way or the highway." It did not take me long to figure out that this organization had no room for individuality or input that was contrary to the self-centered attitude of the owner. He was determined that everything go his way and that his way was the only right way. He asked for suggestions but only wanted answers he liked. He was frustrated that things weren't working but was only interested in his own solutions. If anyone gave opinions that weren't his, he did not accept them. Dysfunctional organizations are secure in being self-centered and forcing the employee culture to conform to their image and likeness.

Dishonesty

Dishonesty is the propaganda that says, "We have no problem." Dishonesty is used to cover up the problem or the truth. The repercussion of dishonesty is that co-dependent employees become liars, covering up truth. There is a dishonesty that permeates a dysfunctional organization because the organization doesn't face the real issue. If the organization does not face the real problem, it will use dishonesty to cover up the fact that nothing is being done about it. "Yes, we realize that we have a problem, and we are working on it." "We are gathering data in order to deal with it."

Co-dependent employees want to believe the propaganda of the cover-up. They want to believe the organization is "working on it," even when months and years go by with no change. Co-dependents have a great ability to numb their feelings in these situations. If they don't acknowledge it or feel it, they can live with it. They are dishonest with themselves by reinforcing organizational dishonesty. If everyone believes a lie, it becomes the truth, even though it is a false "truth."

Perfectionism

In the midst of crisis, confusion and ignoring the real problem, the organization pursues perfection.

Doing one's best is different from perfection. Perfectionism sets employees up for failure because they must push, push, push but can never attain fulfillment. No wonder employees get physically exhausted, emotionally depleted and burned out. Perfectionism is contrary to human nature. Human beings can do excellent work and achieve great things, but perfectionism sets one up for failure. Failure occurs and perpetuates the individual's low self-image. The person tries harder and fails again. It is a vicious cycle. Doing one's best is never good enough in the dysfunctional pursuit of perfection.

In a dysfunctional organization, one way to keep eyes off the real problem is to press employees for perfection. "You shouldn't have time to worry about this. If you had your report in, you wouldn't have time to look at this, and you wouldn't have time to talk about it." Pursuing perfection keeps employees running on the treadmill.

The dysfunctional organization exhausts employees in their pursuit of perfection. Employees don't have the strength to speak up or change the situation. They are striving to measure up to an unattainable yardstick. Soon, the employees discount their own achievements because they are not perfect.

Control

Another major component of a dysfunctional organization involves control. The organization controls its employees by expecting them to act and think as the organization wants. Control is maintained by employees going along with "the way it is." Co-dependent employees knowing how to walk the walk and talk the talk of dysfunction naturally lock into this system.

To lose control heightens the organization's fear. A dysfunctional organization's security lies in exercising full control over everyone and everything in the organization. If the organization believes it is losing control, management tightens control.

The "Carrot Promise"

Dysfunctional organizations keep employees pressing on with the wonderful "carrot promise." "Just hang in there. It's going to come through. We're almost there. It's going to get better." In real life, people and companies go through rough times. There are hectic seasons and rough periods. But if the problem is unresolved and becomes a way of life, the organizaon remains dysfunctional. At one time I was teaching in a college where there had not been any job descriptions for over three years. Everybody was going to get pay increases when all these job descriptions were completed. The promise keeps the employees going. Employees want to believe the propaganda. When something's not quite right and the facts don't add up, employees keep discounting it because they want to believe the wonderful story they are being told. They want to believe the "carrot promise," even when results are not evident.

Is that "carrot" an illusion or reality? If the problem is not dealt with, the "carrot" is going to continue the illusion. To encourage the employees to put up with the problem, the "carrot" is continually dangled. Co-dependent employees believe the "carrot promise" instead of the daily reality of dysfunction.

Invalidation of Viewpoints

A dysfunctional organization invalidates an employee's viewpoint. If the individual's viewpoint isn't the same as the dysfunctional organization, it will not be validated. The employee will be considered a troublemaker. The organization will say, "Oh, you're wrong. What are you talking about?" Then co-workers will say, "You're wrong. What are you talking about?" Pretty soon the employee thinks, "I'm wrong. What am I talking about?" Outside assistance is needed for a reality check.

Dualism

Black-and-white rules make clear what is and isn't accepted in a dysfunctional organization. By following the rules, employees believe they will be safe. If employees try to live in or talk about gray areas, they will be censored. Dysfunctional organizations are inflexible when it comes to dualism. Black-and-white rules constrict individuality and creativity. These rules fortify the control of the dysfunctional organization over employees' beliefs and behaviors.

Branding

If employees speak contrary to the organization's policie and philosophy, they're considered disloyal and *not* tea players. A brand will be placed on the employee, which will k used to discount his input and viewpoints, no matter how accu rate his information. If an employee cannot be trusted to agre with dysfunction, he will be branded. Often, speaking the tru in a dysfunctional organization will result in the brand of a "di loyal employee."

THE PROGRESSION IN DYSFUNCTIONAL ORGANIZATION!

Many dysfunctional organizations are productive and finar cially successful, which reinforces their assessment that nothir is wrong. Even in companies where there is extreme employe dissatisfaction, stress, burnout and turnover, the attitude is th "the job is getting done."

Most organizations do not face the fact that there is a prol lem until there is extreme discomfort in day-to-day activitie and productivity is being negatively affected.

The following describes the progression of stages a dysfun tional organization will experience if intervention does not occu

Stage 1: Denial

At the denial stage the organization experiences an unde current of unrest, yet overall the employees are coping with th situation, maintaining the illusion that everything is "just fine.

Denial signs and symptoms:

- The organization is numb to what the true problem is.

- The organization is embarrassed and avoids facing the trut at all costs.

- Alibis and excuses are generated by management and staff

Organization members feel disloyal when they discuss the problem.

Organization relationships show strain, and a "perfect organization" illusion is created.

Organization members deny problems in the face of real data; incongruent responses are given when they are confronted with the problem.

Stage 2: Elimination

Superficial attempts are made to solve the problem. Symptoms are treated while the real problem is avoided.

Elimination signs and symptoms:

Some external resource is sought to rectify the problem (e.g. consultants, trainers, new incentives, etc.).

Cover-ups are coupled with complex rationales.

A trial-and-error method of problem-solving is initiated.

Attempts are made to maintain illusion. Confusion and uncertainty increase.

Stage 3: Disorganization

Tension is rising at this stage. Even key employees are starting to speak up, trying to address the problem. Management reacts by applying more control. Employees become more resistant.

Disorganization signs and symptoms:

Social adjustment problems are noted in key employees.

Irrational controls are exercised by management. Rebellion in staff is noted and punished.

Survival roles develop. Co-dependency and counterdependency increase.

Managers feel helpless and trapped but report control.

Stage 4: Reorganization

The organization admits that a problem exists and decides that the solution is to reorganize. The office on the north side of the building moves to the south side. Managers are shifted to different departments. Employees are relocated and job responsibilities are redefined. Yet dysfunction, co-dependency and counterdependency are not addressed. Most dysfunctional organizations do all they can to maintain a holding pattern at this stage.

Reorganization signs and symptoms:

- Hope is generated. Relief is briefly experienced.

- Behaviors coincide with demands or are so interpreted.

- The organization admits difficulty.

Stage 5: Escape or Recovery

By this stage the organization and employees are desperate. The pressure and stress have reached a crisis point: if there is no radical change, the last option is to leave. Pressure from outside by the legal system, business community and/or professional affiliations calls attention to the problem that has become blatant.

At this stage many organizations are not able to change because so much damage has been done. All resources for coping with the situation have been depleted in order to survive the dysfunction. Some organizations (and the powers that be in those organizations) hold tight to denial of the problem, no matter what the cost, even the death of the organization.

Escape or recovery signs and symptoms:

- The organization and its employees are torn. There is acknowledgment that either change must occur or one must leave the organization.

- Outside pressure becomes a dominant theme.

- The organization is unable to take constructive action. Magic is required.

- The organization and its employees take action to escape or recover.

THE HEALTHY ORGANIZATION

Healthy organizations are aggressive in maintaining an environment that is positive for the employee culture and organizational growth. Organizations that are serious about maintaining a leading edge into the next millennium are active in pursuing these concepts.

With the employee population drastically shrinking, this issue has become even more crucial. To maintain a solid workforce into the next century, organizations will have to attract and retain employees with more than money. Money is not enough, because employees now want personal and professional fulfillment in their work.

The healthy organizational approach is a win-win attitude for both employee and organization. Healthy beliefs and behaviors are reflected throughout the organization and are a genuine verification of the status of the informal organization.

The following behaviors are indicative of a healthy organization that promotes interdependency between management and staff.

BEHAVIORS IN HEALTHY ORGANIZATIONS

1. Direct, Clear, Open and Productive Communication
2. Identification and Solution of Problems
3. Consistency and Balance
4. Honesty

5. Ethics
6. Value and Respect for Individuals
7. Making Allowances for Mistakes
8. Encouragement of Freedom of Expression
9. Assuming Responsibility for Negative and Positive Actions
10. Validating Self-Worth of Employees
11. Flexible Rules
12. Authentic Work Relationships
13. Encouragement of Creativity

Direct, Clear, Open and Productive Communication

This kind of communication is based on honesty, and it results in action. It is encouraged at all levels, top-to-bottom and bottom-to-top.

Employees are kept abreast of the pertinent information to perform their jobs and the results of those efforts. In a dysfunctional organization, communication is one-way or nonexistent. Open, productive communication should result for both staff and organization in this interaction.

Healthy organizations get to the point with employees by being direct. They minimize employee manipulation by clearly stating the expectations and objectives of the organization. Specific communication defines the responsibilities of any given project and the guidelines needed in meeting the project deadline.

This kind of communication will eliminate comments like "I thought you meant . . ." and "Oh, did you mean me?" from staff vocabulary.

Direct, clear and specific communication makes the sender and receiver accountable. A developed, agreed-upon method of communication streamlines communication and produces growth.

Identification and Solution of Problems

In a healthy organization, problems are addressed. The organization admits the existence of a problem and identifies it. In a dysfunctional organization, management sometimes identifies the problem but doesn't take the needed action to resolve the real problem.

In a healthy organization, one hears, "We've got a problem. What can we do?" This doesn't mean a healthy organization can make all its problems go away. Sometimes problems stay—low budgets, economic structures, seasonal impact, etc. If the problem has an area that cannot be resolved, at least the healthy organization can solve the problem as much as possible. It addresses the problem and decides what can and cannot be done about it, while implementing change accordingly.

In healthy organizations, employees are told, "Yes, we have this problem. This is what we can do with it; this is what we can't do." Employees are able to be more committed to dealing with problems using this process. When employees can speak about and deal with problems honestly, morale is increased. Employees are empowered instead of becoming powerless. The healthy organization deals with the problem instead of ignoring it or applying superficial remedies that ultimately disease the organization.

Consistency and Balance

Instead of crisis and confusion, a healthy organization maintains consistency and balance.

Employees know what is expected of them. There are established ways to perform tasks and fulfill job requirements.

The environment is consistent and balanced, which produces a safe environment in which to work. This is in contrast to the daily minefield of unpredictability in a dysfunctional organization. Sometimes Murphy's Law is active even in a healthy work environment. There are emergency deadlines and unforeseen events that take place. The difference is that in a healthy environment, that is the exception, not the rule.

Honesty

Honesty in a healthy organization is demonstrated by staff not having to guess what is really going on. Honesty also means that truth can be spoken and employees will not be punished for it.

Honest communication in a healthy organization should promote growth. This honesty does not mean that everyone knows everything. Healthy honesty has boundaries as to what is appropriate for management to inform employees of without deception and unethical practices.

Honesty increases the level of trust and commitment within the organization.

Ethics

Ethics are the values that determine how an organization treats its employees and conducts business.

Healthy organizations have ethical values that are stated in their mission statement, declared values and policy/procedure manuals. Ethical practices are demonstrated in dealing with staff and customers on a daily basis. The healthy organization reaffirms the ethical approach in dealing with staff, in providing services and in all facets of operating the organization.

Value and Respect for Individuals

Healthy organizations value and respect employees. They appreciate their contribution to the organization. They see the employee as the most valuable asset of the organization. Treating employees with respect can be one of the most important attributes of an organization.

Employees will "go the distance" for an organization that values and respects them.

Making Allowances for Mistakes

A healthy organization makes room for mistakes. Human beings make mistakes. A healthy organization can handle that. Employees should do the best job they can and fulfill the responsibilities of their positions. Mistakes that haunt employees for the rest of their careers are destructive to employees and the organization. Employees need to learn from mistakes, take responsibility for mistakes and grow from mistakes.

Encouragement of Freedom of Expression

Healthy organizations sincerely encourage employee feedback. This doesn't mean freedom to constantly vent frustrations inappropriately. Freedom of expression means the employees share their viewpoints. Organizations can gain a tremendous amount of information from employees who feel positive or negative about an issue. Even a very negative opinion will have some important aspects to consider. With the goal of the organization as the focus, freedom of expression should assist in attaining that goal.

Assuming Responsibility for Negative and Positive Actions

A healthy organization takes responsibility for positive and negative actions. If positive things happen, recognition is given. If something negative happens, it's acknowledged and dealt with, and the organization moves on from the experience.

In a major company, a gigantic blunder had been made. All the employees had been working overtime and double shifts to complete the deadline of this major project, and then it flopped. It turned out to be a total waste of time and money.

Everyone knew it, but it was never spoken about openly in the organization. Yes, it was an embarrassing situation for the organization, but what did it learn from this experience? Valuable information can be learned from negative experiences. Organizations can gain strength and commitment to move forward if they take responsibility for the positive as well as the negative. Organizations not taking responsibility for the negative perpetuate dishonesty, which in time could lead to unethical and illegal practices.

Validating Self-Worth of Employees

The self-worth of the employee is validated when the organization treats the employee as a worthwhile person instead of a worthless person. Self-worth is also validated when the organization invests in the employee to groom her talents and abilities for personal and professional enhancement. Even when the employee falls short of the organization's expectations, self-worth continues being validated. Expectations of the employee should be addressed without voiding the employee's self-worth. Self-worth is personal, not performance.

If a circumstance occurs and the employee must be terminated, focus should be put on lack of performance, not lack of personal worth. An employee can be terminated while self-worth is validated.

Flexible Rules

Dysfunctional organizations are in a straightjacket of black-and-white rules. Management within a healthy organization is conscious of the human condition. Management realizes the best way to effectively deal with human beings is to be flexible yet focused on the goal of the organization. Humans need humane rules that are flexible and considerate of life conditions, yet are ethically in tune with all employees and organizational focus.

Rules can change within reason in a healthy organization. This attitude will assist the organization in adapting to growth and change.

Authentic Work Relationships

Healthy organizations build authentic work relationships. Authenticity stops game-playing so the work relationship can develop a real and sincere depth of connection among employees. Instead of supporting a superficial facade, these authentic work relationships create an environment of genuine support.

Encouragement of Creativity

Creativity abounds when employees are living in an environment that reduces fear, mistrust, anger, stress and burnout. It supports, validates and encourages staff to be all they can be.

Encouragement of creativity provides growth and expansion for the employee as well as the organization that wants to stay on the cutting edge of an ever-changing marketplace.

OPERATING SYSTEMS

Areas	Healthy Functioning	Dysfunctioning
Communications	Direct	Indirect
	Clear	Unclear
	Specific	Vague
	Congruent	Incongruent
Rules	Overt	Covert
	Up-to-Date	Out-of-Date
	Humane	Inhumane
	Flexible	Rigid

Areas	Healthy Functioning	Dysfunctioning
Employee Self-Worth	High: Confidence	Low: No Confidence
Work Relationships	Interdependence	Extreme Dependence or Independence
Change	Creative Compromising Involved Balanced Growth-Producing	Forced Blaming Detached Distracted Growth-Impeding
Outcome	Realistic Ordered Appropriate Constructive	Accidental Chaotic Inappropriate Destructive

Every organization has an operating system with some degree of health and dysfunction. Left unattended, organizations are in danger of being eroded by the disease of dysfunction.

INTERDEPENDENCY

Interdependency is the trait of an organization whose employee culture is able to exercise individual identity and corporate expression. Each employee is a "piece" that is valued on its own yet is completed in expression when connected to the other pieces.

Like links of a chain, each link has an independent expression of individual strength while being dependent on the other links for the expression of the chain.

The foundation of interdependency is built on respect—respect for individual employee value and respect for all employee value. I'm afraid there would never be a chain if the individual links did not respect their own strength or did not respect the strength of the other links.

A theme that runs rampant in dysfunctional organizations is no respect for staff or management. Without respect, trust is impossible. Distrust alienates employees from each other. Territories are protected by overt and covert aggressive tactics. Fierce independence or crippling dependence are the norm.

In Stephen Covey's book, *The Seven Habits of Highly Effective People*, he points out the paradigm shift of moving from dependence to independence to the ultimate goal of interdependence. Before a person can attain true independence—which is not isolation—and move into authentic interdependency, the dysfunctional cycle of co-dependency/counterdependency must be broken.

Interdependence is the balance of healthy independence and healthy dependence. Being independent is the ability to take responsibility for your "piece." Healthy dependence is relying on the contribution of fellow employees to complete your piece in a corporate expression.

An employee who is interdependent can stand separately or together in the responsibility of his position. Boundaries are clear, and individuality is not lost in either stance.

Interdependency Building Blocks

For an employee culture to attain interdependence, there are four necessary building blocks:

1. Communication: Knock on the door.
2. Respect: Open the door.
3. Trust: Step in the door.
4. Commitment: Stay for interaction.

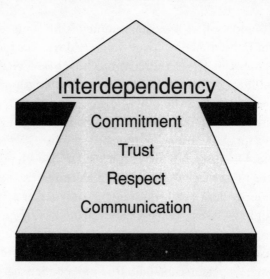

Communication: Knock on the door. Provide communication skills training. The Myers-Briggs or the Personal Profile System™ Inventory are excellent instruments to assist employees in learning their own communication style and the traits of coworkers' communication styles. In this way, the practical steps of how to approach employees in problem-solving, implementing change, motivation and conflict resolution can be learned and practiced.

The foundation of communication is also necessary to provide an environment where unresolved historical issues or employee disputes can be resolved. It is sometimes advisable to have a facilitator who is skilled in conflict resolution supervise this process.

By resolving historical issues, the organization is able to function from a healthier foundation.

With a healthier foundation, communication keeps the "air clear" by resolving conflict issues as they arise.

If there is no attempt to resolve "old wounds," the next step will not be possible.

Respect: Open the door. By opening up communication and learning about individual communication style, employees will begin to respect their own style, as well as to respect others. Some of the mystery of why people act the way they do will be discovered. Confidence in dealing with co-workers will increase. Assertive skills will fortify healthier behavior and decrease co-dependent/counterdependent behaviors. Respect takes root by providing an environment that keeps communication open. Employees get to know their own and co-workers' communication styles. Skills necessary to express self and listen to others are developed.

When employees have low self-esteem, they don't respect themselves, and in turn hold others in contempt (counter-dependent aggressive protection). Or they may placate others (co-dependent passive protection). By establishing healthy communication, self-respect and mutual respect the cycle of dysfunction will be disrupted.

Mutual respect in a healthy organization is experienced on all levels, top-to-bottom and bottom-to-top.

Trust: Step in the door. Trust takes time—time to test how secure the work environment is, if communication is honest, if respect is genuine, and if it is safe to risk. Gaining trust is not easy, since most employees have learned through damaging lessons not to trust.

Once trust is established, employees are willing to invest in a committed work relationship with co-workers and the organization.

Trust occurs when employees know they can believe what they are told and do not have to guess what is really being said. Trust occurs when employees feel they can speak up and will not be punished. Trust is knowing that no matter what the misunderstanding or upsetting situation that might occur, there are healthy avenues to resolve these issues with respect and integrity.

Commitment: Stay for interaction. With communication, respect and trust, commitment to interact is the next step. If commitment is lacking in a department or organization, there is a problem with the first three building blocks. Most organizations want committed employees. They believe the employee should be committed to the mission and goal of the organization. The employees may believe in the mission and *want* to attain the goal of the organization. However, if the first three elements are not a reality, employees will be committed only to protecting themselves and surviving the duration of their employment.

When employees believe in two-way communication, experience the respect of self and others, and trust the work relationship, they are eager to commit themselves to the life of the organization, not just existence in the organization.

Interdependency is cultivated in healthy work relationships that demonstrate communication, respect, trust and commitment. Interdependency, based on these four building blocks, will be evident throughout the organization. After having established and fortified the four building blocks of interdependence, the outcome should be experienced in these 10 components:

1. Communication is top-to-bottom and bottom-to-top.

2. Staff has an opportunity for "input" in the decision-making process of management.

3. The individual is responsible for his/her position in an effort to meet the goal of the department/organization.

4. All employees are treated with respect and dignity.

5. All employees are accountable for their position and productivity.

6. Management and staff are willing to speak the truth.

7. Management and staff are committed to increase personal and professional skills.

8. Management and staff are flexible in the change and growth of the organization.

9. Mutual trust exists between management and staff.

10. The work environment reflects individual and corporate commitment.

Interdependent work relationships among staff and management will increase morale and productivity. The health of the organization will be fortified, and dysfunction will be minimized.

Co-dependent/counterdependent work relationships cannot be maintained in a healthy organization that has an interdependent employee culture.

Chapter 5

The Transformation at Work

The foundation for a healthy organization is laid by establishing healthy work relationships and a healthy work environment. To establish a healthy organization, there must be a commitment to the Healthy Change Process. The Healthy Change Process is necessary to make the fundamental impact on the informal organization that is the cultural structure of the organization. Establishing healthy functioning must be promoted on two levels: one, the employee as an individual and co-worker; and two, the organization as a whole.

Herman Miller Inc. is a furniture company founded in 1923. In 1983 it was chosen as one of the 100 best companies to work for in America. A hundred dollars invested in stock in 1975 had grown in value to $4,854.60 in 1986 (41% rate of growth). In 1988 *Fortune* picked Herman Miller Inc. as one of the nation's "ten most admired companies." The company was ranked fourth out of all U.S. companies in the category of "quality of products or services." This company's chief executive officer, Max Depree (son of the founder D.J. Depree), states in his book, *Leadership Is an Art*, that "Effective influencing and understanding spring largely from healthy relationships among the members of the group. Leaders need to foster environments and work processes within which people can develop high-quality relationships—relationships with each other, relationships with the group with which we work, relationships with our clients and customers."

THE HEALTHY CHANGE PROCESS

Before organizational health can be established, the organization (employee) must first realize there is dysfunction that needs to be discontinued.

Usually, by the time an organization (employee) decides to discontinue dysfunctional behaviors, the tolerance for this kind of lifestyle has been exhausted. Only after numerous attempts to successfully live with dysfunction have proven futile is there a willingness to attempt an alternative solution. The organization (employee) is hopeful that there is a better, healthier way, yet there is no personal experience of what that is or how to attain it.

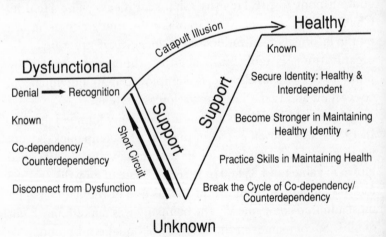

In the beginning of the Healthy Change Process, the organization (employee) has moved from denial of the problem into recognizing that life as they know it is dysfunctional.

At this stage, the relationships are based on co-dependent/counterdependent beliefs and behaviors.

There is a known conformity of what is acceptable behavior within the dysfunctional environment.

The organization (employee) wants to make the situation better.

They are hopeful that by learning about dysfunction and co-dependency they will be able to change. They decide to choose healthier behaviors. They expect to have instant results by mental determination.

An important factor to remember is that healthy change is a *process*! It is not a mental decision. It is not possible to instantly catapult (catapult illusion) out of dysfunction into healthy beliefs and behaviors.

During the Healthy Change Process, instead of being catapulted into a higher level of health, the opposite proves true. The organization (employee) experiences that things get worse instead of better. They wonder, "What has happened? Here I am trying to make things better and it is worse than ever!" At this point if the organization (employee) does not understand the Healthy Change Process, it will return to (short-circuit) dysfunction. It is important to understand the crucial issues that are in play at this stage in order to continue the Healthy Change Process.

When an organization (employee) has lived in dysfunction, that is the only way it knows how to live. This may be depleting emotionally, physically and financially, but it is familiar. To start to change this dysfunctional behavior, an organization (employee) must first stop participating in the dysfunction. By attempting to discontinue dysfunctional/co-dependent behaviors the organization (employee) is propelled into an unknown area. Unfortunately, the organization (employee) doesn't have a handle on how to be healthy. This start is like stepping off the face of the earth into the unknown void. One client referred to it as "riding on the elevator to hell." This void of the unknown fills people with fear and terror. The anxiety of "What will happen to me?" becomes overwhelming. At this point, inside fear is activated, and outside circumstances start to cause increased problems.

For example, an employee realizes that due to her co-dependent behavior she has neglected to take her own lunch breaks in order to cover everyone else's lunch breaks. The employee decides she will increase healthy behavior and reduce her co-dependency by taking her lunch breaks. Even though this would seem to be a simple and logical approach, the outcome could be as follows: The employee has experienced some fear in speaking up for herself and requesting a lunch break. The outside environment of co-workers will react to this change. The co-workers have been accustomed to her covering all the lunches, but now they will have to take a turn. They may become angry or resentful. This reaction from the outside will impact the employee. She will feel that a lunch break is not worth having co-workers upset with her. Here she was trying to improve her behavior, and things got worse. So, instead of working through the inside fear and the outside upset of co-workers, she goes back (short-circuits) to how things always were, the known. This is a simple example, but the dynamics are the same for employees or organizations in the Healthy Change Process.

Until the organization (employee) is exhausted from dysfunction and the short-circuit approach, further progress in the process of attaining a healthier lifestyle will not be made.

Support is an important component of successfully working through the void of the unknown and establishing healthy beliefs and behaviors. One needs the support of people and consultants who have gone through the process of healthy change and have experienced implementing a healthy lifestyle personally and professionally. Support persons are those people who know the stages of the Healthy Change Process and the skills to live it.

Support fortifies the organization (employee) to continue the process of healthy change when things seemingly get worse before they get better. Support assists in lowering fear and anxiety during this time of change by focusing the organization (employee) on the goal of attaining healthy behaviors.

As the organization (employee) disconnects from dysfunction, skills to implement healthy change need to be established and maintained.

During the continued process of healthy change, the organization (employee) will become stronger in a healthier identity. In time, healthy beliefs and behaviors will be the norm. The known will be a secure identity in being healthy and interdependent.

BREAKING THE CYCLE OF THE CO-DEPENDENT/COUNTER-DEPENDENT EMPLOYEE

During the Healthy Change Process, employees need to implement the following eight items to assist in breaking the cycle of co-dependency/counterdependency:

1. Read books and attend workshops on dysfunction and co-dependency/counterdependency.

2. Observe and recognize co-dependent/counterdependent beliefs and behaviors at home and at work.

3. End whatever addiction (alcohol, other drugs, gambling, etc.) you use to avoid dealing with your emotions. Seek professional assistance when breaking an addictive behavior. Twelve-step meetings such as Alcoholics Anonymous, Narcotics Anonymous and Overeaters Anonymous are an excellent way to assist an individual with the recovery process.

4. Find support with people who have dealt with their own co-dependency/counterdependency. Their lives should reflect these changes at home and at work.

5. Move according to your own speed. It takes patience an practice to establish your feelings, thoughts and true self

6. Be considerate of yourself in decision-making. "What do expect from others and myself? What are my boundaries?"

7. Be considerate of others during the change process withou forfeiting self.

8. Celebrate your successes, no matter how small. Share thes experiences with people who are supportive of your pe sonal and professional growth.

Remember, breaking a lifelong cycle can be confusing an uncomfortable until your true self becomes your reality!

ISSUES IN HEALTHY CHANGE FOR CO-DEPENDENT EMPLOYEES

The following items will assist the Wonderful Worke Angry Avenger, Chameleon, Joker and Talking Head to imple ment healthy beliefs and behaviors in their personal and pro fessional lives:

Wonderful Worker

1. Learn to "let go" and not control others in the workplace

2. Find and express repressed feelings of weakness, helplessness and doubt in a supportive environment.

3. Learn to relax and not overextend on projects.

4. Learn to accept failure or mistakes.

5. Learn to accept self as lovable, not based on achievemen

6. Learn to ask for and accept help from co-workers and supervisors.

7. Learn to be a kid again, spontaneous and playful.

8. Learn to satisfy your own needs first, at home and at work.

9. Take care of your physical needs.

10. Capitalize on "responsibility" in a healthy and positive way.

Angry Avenger

1. Identify anger and rage and learn appropriate ways to express them.

2. Focus on "real problems" and accept that "they" are not the problem.

3. Accept responsibility for self as a person and professional.

4. Accept self as someone of value in the workplace.

5. Learn to identify and express feelings to co-workers and supervisors.

6. Identify self as an individual, not as an extension of the organization.

7. Learn to identify and express needs of self at home and at work.

8. Learn to respect people in authority.

9. Learn to interact with others in healthy ways in the workplace.

Chameleon

1. Learn to accept positive attention and recognition.

2. Learn to constructively resolve conflicts in the workplace.

3. Learn to express wants and needs directly to co-workers and supervisors.

4. Learn to express feelings, especially anger, directly and appropriately.

5. Learn to identify your own power of choices and decision-making.

6. Learn to accept responsibility for self as a person and professional.

7. Learn to interact with co-workers and supervisors.

8. Learn to lead, not always follow, staff members.

9. Capitalize on independency, flexibility and creativity.

Joker

1. Recognize your own sanity.

2. Learn not to take on the responsibility for stress of co-workers or the organization.

3. Learn to take self more seriously as a professional.

4. Learn to identify and express feelings appropriately.

5. Accept responsibility for position and professional contribution.

6. Become more independent of co-workers' distress.

7. Learn to slow down and relax.

8. Learn to identify and express needs in the workplace.

9. Learn to take care of self.

10. Learn to receive help from co-workers and supervisors.

Talking Head

1. Learn to identify and feel feelings.

2. Attach feelings to analytical process.

3. Learn to have fun and laugh.

4. Learn not to take self so seriously.

5. Learn to flow with life under less structure.

6. Learn to ask for help from co-workers and supervisors.

7. Learn to have variety in life.

8. Practice spontaneity.

9. Be in touch with physical limits.

BREAKING THE CYCLE: CREATING HEALTHY CHANGE

Every organization has co-dependent/counterdependent employees promoting and fortifying dysfunction. To implement healthy change, the cycle of dysfunction has to be broken. There are 10 practical steps that can increase healthy behavior while minimizing dysfunction.

1. *Set up guidelines of employee responsibility.* Guidelines clarify what the employee is responsible for in his job description.

   Guidelines are boundaries that minimize the tendency of co-dependent employees to take on co-workers' job duties. These boundaries also limit the controlling counter-dependent employees from intruding into other employees' areas of responsibility.

   A recent scientific study observed elementary school children at play during recess. When the play area was fenced, children used the entire area, including bouncing balls against the fence. When the fence was removed, the children played closer to the school building and did not venture out.

   This is a simple representation of what happens when employees have boundaries and guidelines. They are free to use their whole area with confidence.

2. *Practice assertive behavior.* Basic assertiveness training can assist in minimizing passive and aggressive behavior. Assertiveness gives the employees skills in developing interdependent behaviors. Boundaries are set and maintained by assertive behavior, which is healthy for both employee and organization.

3. *Support self and others through the discovery of healthy behavior.* When resolving dysfunction and experiencing the Healthy Change Process, there is uncertainty and awkwardness.

Support yourself and others during this time and allow the process to take place.

4. *Encourage communication, both positive and negative.* By appropriate open communication, issues can be resolved and growth can and will take place. If you can get mad, you can get glad. Both positive and negative communication is necessary to maintain balance in personal and professional life while breaking the cycle of dysfunction.

5. *Keep each employee informed of accountability and responsibility.* It is important not to drop the ball when change is taking place. It takes repetition to discontinue dysfunctional practices and implement healthy behavior. By keeping employees informed of accountability and responsibility, consistency and balance is ongoing.

6. *Let employees experience the benefits and consequences of their behavior.* Healthy organizations support both benefits and consequences of employee behavior. A crucial part of breaking the cycle of dysfunction is to minimize enabling behavior. Co-dependent employees enable by protecting co-workers, managers, etc., from the consequences of irresponsible/ inappropriate behavior.

   To be balanced and healthy, employees need both sides of the lessons life teaches. Behaviors have positive and negative effects on our personal and professional lives. Learning to grow from each experience is the real lesson.

7. *Give private and public recognition of employees' accomplishment and extra effort.* To strengthen the degree of health in the organization, employee recognition should become a natural part of interaction between management and staff. When employees don't receive recognition for their accomplishments, the fiber of the organization is weakened.

8. *Restrict employees in "going overboard" in prolonged work hours and taking work home.* Keeping employees healthy keeps the organization healthy. Work addiction promotes co-dependent

counterdependent work relationships and is physically and emotionally devastating for top-notch employees. Protect high-achieving employees by establishing boundaries on work hours. Bryan Robinson's book, *Work Addiction: Hidden Legacies of Adult Children*, explains the effect of work addiction on a person's work and family.

9. *Promote the employee and organizational goal of balance in work, family, play and self.* Balance for the employee in the four areas of work, family, play and self is necessary to ensure years of healthy consistent productivity. The organization should be the leader in promoting resources (training, education, services, etc.) that assist employees in learning about and implementing healthy lifestyles at work, home, play and with self.

10. *Encourage employees to invest in physical, mental, emotional and spiritual well-being.* Encourage employees to use resources available through the organization or in the community to enhance quality in their personal and professional lives.

MAINTAINING ORGANIZATIONAL AND EMPLOYEE HEALTH

Establishing a healthy foundation, though essential, is not enough, just as laying the foundation and building a new industrial complex is not enough without maintenance. In time, weeds and decay will take over. Maintaining organizational health is needed to cultivate and groom a healthy work environment that minimizes dysfunction and promotes the continuing process of healthy work relationships.

Set up a support structure that will alert you as to the health and dysfunction of the department/organization. The support structure should also make available resources to ensure the health of the employee culture and organizational environment.

Remember that an organization is a living organism that needs continuing growth and development to maintain a high level of health.

The following are basic structures and systems that ensure a healthy organization:

Support Structures

Contact trained consultants with expertise in:

- Organizational development
- Dysfunctional systems
- Co-dependency/counterdependency

Conduct in-service workshops on:

- Communication skills
- Dysfunctional organizations/healthy organizations
- Co-dependency in the workplace
- Healthy organizations and interdependency
- Balancing work, family and community

Use the resources of Employee Assistance Programs (EAP). The EAP is staffed with counselors skilled in addictions and co-dependency issues, and it has community resources for employees to use in gaining assistance with personal and professional co-dependency issues.

Provide information and resources for employees' well-being, such as stress reduction, time management, etc.

Establish resource library on site. Make materials available that address addiction, dysfunction, co-dependency and how to balance one's life in a variety of areas.

Institute organizational play time, relaxation and social interaction. This should be made available but not mandatory.

Provide some flexibility to the work schedule, such as:

- Four-day work week (10 hours per day, 40 hours per week)
- Flextime (Adjustable work schedule)
- Job share (Two people share one position)

- Flexplace (Provide a portion of work that can be done at work or at home. Computers make this a viable option.)
- Establish "work-hour boundaries" that minimize work addiction and burnout.
- Encourage employee input to job creativity and productivity.

Monitoring Systems

On a regular basis (every six months to one year) have an organizational-development consultant perform an organizational analysis to determine the health of the organization and its departments.

Monitor:
- Employee productivity
- Employee morale/job satisfaction
- Turnover
- Growth of the company
- Workers' compensation claims and progress
- Community image

Ask these questions often:
- Is interdependent management taking place?
- Is the support structure thriving with life or being used as an oasis?
- Is new, exciting, productive growth happening?
- Is the organization boldly expressing its mission and values and the characteristics of a healthy organization?

It is vitally important that business large and small worldwide become aware of the value of investing in its human resources.

Organizations are living organisms made up of people. This living organism functions from a foundation of health or a foundation of dysfunction.

Dysfunctional family systems destroy the family and its members. Dysfunctional organizations destroy the organization and the employee culture.

Healthy family systems strengthen the family and its members. Healthy organizations strengthen the growth and productivity of the organization, employees and community.

To affect the bottom-line results of productivity, the root issues of dysfunction need to be courageously addressed and healthy change implemented.

In the future, the focus of organizations that are on the cutting edge of national and international competition will need to be directed to the health of the organization and the health of the employee culture. Without this fundamental emphasis on health, the disease of dysfunction will weaken and cripple the foundation of corporate culture.

One Woman's Story

Twenty-five years ago Katie was fresh out of college and unsure of what she wanted for a career.

Her first job was with a nationally known retail store. Management was impressed with Katie's personal charm, charisma and ability to get the job done, no matter what the deadline.

Katie quickly started up the ranks of the corporate ladder as her marriage to an alcoholic started going down the tubes. The more she felt out of control at home, the more she drove herself for success at work. As the awards, pay raises and professional perks increased, she tried to numb herself to the decline of her marriage by burying herself in work.

Because Katie's 70- to 80-hour workweeks produced outstanding results for the company, she was asked to be vice president of a store in a major city 125 miles from her home. Katie wanted to accept the position even though her husband was not willing to move. She told herself that everything would be fine and that she would be able to handle it because that is what she was used to doing. So she accepted the offer and began overseeing 1,000 employees, working 70 to 80 hours per week and seeing her husband on the weekends.

Before long she found out her husband had been having an affair and wanted a divorce. Katie believed she could fix the situation. If she could run a store with 1,000 employees, surely she could resolve this problem. The Cycle of Hope continued.

After a vacation getaway with her husband, Katie realized that the marriage was over and could not be fixed, yet she was not ready to give up. The Cycle of Hope continued.

Still performing at work at top speed with her ever-present smile and endless energy, Katie did not tell anyone about her problems at home. She continued commuting on the weekends to try to keep the last embers of her marriage alive as she forged ahead. The Cycle of Hope continued.

Katie began to lose her bounce and zip. She reluctantly went to the doctor to see what the problem was. Much to her surprise, the impossible had happened. She was pregnant!

The pregnancy was not well received by her husband, who was now very distant from her emotionally. She knew the only choice for her was to have her child and face the reality of the situation. She kept the pregnancy a secret as long as she could and continued to perform for the company because the company was the one relationship in which she was successful at receiving validation and acceptance.

The birth of her son made Katie take a look at her husband's alcoholism and his continued affair with the other woman. Katie realized that she was a single parent, and she divorced her husband when the baby was three months old. She pulled herself together and got on with her life.

Katie continued her regular 70- to 80-hour workweek in order to prove to everyone that she could do it all. She hired a wonderful nanny to be with her son, and she forged ahead as the vice president of the store. One day on the way home from work she stopped by a grocery store to pick up a few things. She found herself staring at all the choices of salad dressing without being able to decide which one to buy. She was overwhelmed that she could not make a decision. She said to herself, "You are really in bad shape." She left her shopping cart in the aisle and ran out of the store. Driving home she realized she was at a breaking point and had better do something about it.

Beside all the pressures over the years that had brought her to this point, she realized that her primary relationship was now with her two-year-old son and that she needed to re-evaluate her relationship with the company. Her priorities had changed, and she had to change her relationship with the company, too.

This transition was monumental for Katie. Her identity was her position, her life was the store and all her friends were the employees of the store. She would refer to her friends as her "10-minute friends" because she had invested in the friendship 10 minutes at a time over 20 years. She felt deeply connected to them and had no other life outside the life of the store.

After tremendous soul-searching she asked to be removed from the position of vice-president. She was so exhausted that she had not even thought what her next step would be. The president of the company did not want to lose Katie, so he created a new position for her in store management. Much to her surprise the company supported her request to work regular hours with weekends and holidays off. This was unheard of in the retail industry.

Katie was deeply touched by the support of the company and committed to do her best in her new position. Her reputation followed her, and staff expected Katie to continue to be able to follow through with the unending list of requests to get the job done. Katie tried to set boundaries in order to recover from burnout and live a more balanced life. This was very difficult for Katie because she did not want to disappoint anyone or not live up to what was expected of her. Co-workers would cheer her on, saying that they knew she would be back on track and that the vice president position was waiting for her when she was ready. Even though some of the pressure had lessened, she still was trying to live up to the standards of the company and please the people who expected her to be the same old Katie.

She knew the problem was not the store but that she had out-grown that part of her life. She was changing. She needed to be doing more meaningful work that was in balance with the values she was discovering in her new life.

One day she saw a newspaper article reviewing *When Money Is Not Enough* and an upcoming workshop. After reading the article and taking the stress test, which confirmed her level of burnout, she knew she needed more than a workshop. She needed one-on-one to address the personal and professional issues in her life.

Katie was determined to get the answer and fix her life. Much to her surprise the answer was a process, the Healthy Change Process. The first thing she was directed to do was start to create a life for herself so she could find her own identity. She was to join an activity where no one knew who she was. This seemed an impossible task for Katie since she knew most of the prominent people in the city. After attending a choir performance she decided she wanted to sing, so she joined the singing group.

The choral group proved to be the perfect choice. Katie was just one of the singers, and she could practice just singing and being herself. As Katie started expanding her life, working on her co-dependent issues and setting secure boundaries at work she began to realize it was time for her to start looking into other options and career choices. Facing the "void of the unknown" was very frightening to Katie. She had not known any other life outside the store. Katie felt she was being disloyal to the company that had groomed her, rewarded her and stood by her when her marriage fell apart. Having to face leaving the company was more than Katie could bear.

Katie was wrestling with the issues that were facing her when a well-known physician came into her life. To her this seemed like a golden door of opportunity. He gave her expensive gifts, was charming and took an interest in her son. Katie's friends told her how lucky she was to have such a successful and wealthy man come into her life. Everything looked perfect and seemed an answer to her prayers. Now she could gracefully quit her job, be the doctor's wife, take care of her son and do volunteer work.

The charm and the gifts continued as the wedding got closer. Katie's soon-to-be-husband suggested that since he had more than enough money for both of them, she could consolidate her property, savings and investments with his. She felt a bit hesitant but did not want to displease him or seem disloyal.

Not long after the marriage Katie became alarmed by her new husband's emotional issues and the control he had over her. She went back to counseling to try to come to grips with what was going on. With the help of friends and counseling she realized she had made a mistake in getting married for security. Now she needed to work her way out of the problem she found herself in.

After a year of marriage Katie walked away from everything and let go of the financial assets she had given over to her husband's control. This was important for her in order to take control of herself and claim her personal and professional life as her own.

Katie relates her personal relationships to the way she approached her career. She lost her identity in both the personal and professional arena, and the cost was high. By completing the Healthy Change Process, she was able to learn the critical importance of gaining the strength of a healthy interdependent identity in order to fulfill self in personal and professional life.

As she continued the Healthy Change Process, Katie was able to establish an authentic and interdependent lifestyle in her new career as a career coach and a motivational speaker on self-empowerment. Her lifestyle is a balanced blend of personal and professional fulfillment.

One Man's Story

Alex, now 43, was raised in a small rural lumber town. His parents worked at low-wage positions to support the family. They were committed to providing a better life for their children than they had experienced. Because of this dream they created the Idealized American Family profile for their children. Being the oldest of the three children, Alex was groomed to be a Wonderful Worker.

Alex's grandfather had come to the United States from the Old Country, so the family was proud when Alex was the first to go to college. Alex worked very hard to complete college and become a respiratory therapist. The job security and salary that went with the hospital position pleased his parents. He was considered an excellent employee and quickly was given leadership responsibilities in the critical-care units. He knew he excelled in his position, but after ten years the stress was beginning to take its toll on his health and his committed relationship.

Over the last five years of this career he moved up the ranks into management, hoping that he would find some relief from the stress. At first the change seemed to have brought some balance into his life. But because of his co-dependency issues, before long Alex found himself not being able to say no to the continually increasing demands of his job.

Alex felt overly responsible to his position and his patients, and this was costing him his health and his relationship. As the pressures continued, the warning signs of his exhaustion and the disharmony at home were not enough. Not until his relationship ended and an asthma attack put him in the hospital did Alex realize that he was at his limit. Not knowing the real cause of his physical and emotional pain, he decided to leave California.

Alex took four months off after the move to recover from burnout and consider the next step. Because he was familiar only with the known of the hospital environment and needed money, he began working as a temporary respiratory therapist. He thought this would be a way to reduce stress and have financial security. Before too long he realized the repeating pattern and felt he would soon fall victim to the same system that had led to his burnout. In a desperate attempt to escape, he decided that he would become a real-estate agent. He knew that being a real-estate agent was not his ideal career, but he hoped it would give him some freedom and control of his life.

During his first year working as an independent agent, he became disillusioned and fearful. He believed he needed to work as an assistant to a high-volume real-estate agent. Alex felt this would be an opportunity to gain experience and self-confidence as well as financial security.

The woman agent who recruited him as her assistant was very high-powered and controlling. Alex was grateful for the opportunity since he felt unsure about his skill level and realized the real-estate environment was harshly competitive.

Before long Alex found himself doing everything he could to please his boss, hoping that she would realize his worth. Even though her business increased significantly with the skills he brought to the team, he was never recognized or compensated.

Commissions were always dispensed entirely at her discretion and without consistency. He was not able to set his boundaries or maintain them due to her inability to give up her control. He found himself frustrated, exhausted and helpless to change his situation. He could not believe he was back in the same spot after trying so hard to change his life and career. Fear overcame him when he thought of having to face the unknown.

Because history was repeating itself again, he knew he needed to look deeper than the career issues. To get to the source of his repeated dilemma, he was going to have to make significant personal change in order to have lasting effect on his life.

Friends encouraged him to go to counseling and deal with his co-dependency issues in the hopes that his self-esteem would become strong enough that he could take charge of his life and career.

With the help of counseling and the support of his friends, Alex soon began to realize why and how the pattern of co-dependency and burnout kept repeating in his life and his careers. He started to make progress through the Healthy Change Process by discontinuing co-dependent behaviors and integrating interdependent beliefs and behaviors in his life and work. These healthy behaviors were met with strong resistance from his boss. In these encounters he would face the anger of her counterdependency and wonder to himself, "Is this worth it?" When he asked for a fair and consistent commission rate, her reaction was to increase his financial responsibility of her operating cost, resulting in a drastic cut to his basic wage, which he could barely survive on.

As he became stronger in his interdependent skills, a more clearly defined Alex emerged. He recognized that he was in a toxic work environment and that his healthy behaviors were threatening to his employer's counterdependent control. He had no choice but to leave if he wanted to live a more fulfilling life an career in balance with the personal values he had discovered.

With the development of his interdependent skills, his sel esteem had become strong enough to give him the self confidence to set out and create the life he wanted.

After walking through the Healthy Change Process, Ale experienced a new sense of security in himself. He followed hi heart's desire and started a personalized cooking service in th homes of busy professionals. Within six months his reputatio quickly spread and he appeared in the newspaper and on tele vision. Overnight Alex turned his dream into a success, thoug he refers to it as "an overnight, lifetime success."

Alex is committed to his new history of self-fulfillment an career satisfaction. Interdependency and balance in life is a dail focus for Alex and his cooking crew.

With the personal and professional success Alex is experi encing, he plans to incorporate interdependent principles in th "Personalized Chef Cooking Course" he is in the process o developing.

One Company's Story

Benge Construction Co., of Wilsonville, Oregon, was started ten years ago by owner Scott Benge after much consideration as to what would be the stabilizing factors for his business.

During the previous 14 years, Scott had been involved in a family-owned construction business that had fallen on hard times due to family problems and Oregon's recession in the early '80s.

Being the oldest of three brothers and the Wonderful Worker of the family business, Scott felt extremely responsible when the family business went under. Even though intellectually he knew that the factors which led to the closure of the business were beyond his control, the shame and guilt stayed with him.

After the failure of the family business, Scott was hired as a controller for a local contractor. It did not take him long to realize that he had no tolerance for a controlling and demanding boss. The counterdependent boss did not show him basic respect or make him feel valued. Scott knew that this kind of treatment was typical of the hard-line attitude in the construction field. In Scott's heart he believed that if employees were treated with respect and dignity, not only would they get the job done, but the employees would experience personal and professional fulfillment.

Scott found another contractor who was willing to hire him as a part-time estimator so he could start some contract work on his own. As he worked at his own contracts, the ghosts of the past would visit him. Often he wondered if having his own business would be worth it. Could he really do it differently?

Scott had a few good friends at the Association of General Contractors (AGC) who kept encouraging him with stories of some of the legends in the construction field who had lost everything and were able to start over and succeed in a bigger and better way with perseverance. Scott was encouraged by these stories of success as he began to build his own construction company. But he knew he needed more than perseverance. He just was not sure what "more" was.

Due to his ethnic heritage, Scott was able to qualify for minority status with the Small Business Administration. This was another piece, Scott believed, that would secure the foundation of his business during the start-up phase. Dealing with his ethnicity was also another avenue for him to discover and claim his identity.

He and his wife, Joan, had been looking for a church to attend when they were told about the Living Enrichment Center. As they became involved with the church, Scott was inspired by the ministers' message. He wanted to aspire to the personal and spiritual values of wholeness in both his personal and professional lives.

Scott started realizing that he needed the stabilizing factor of personal growth in his professional life more than perseverance. He had begun to see that his behaviors to please others to the point of exhaustion were co-dependent and would be detrimental in running his business. Signs of that were showing up already with his feeling overly responsible for his employees and their family members. This feeling would often influence his decision-making more than sound business practices would

ictate. On occasion counterdependent contractors would in-
imidate his better judgment in negotiations.

He had become aware that if he was truly going to make a
ositive difference in his life and his business, he would have to
eal with the core issues of co-dependency. During this time of
elf-assessment, Scott contracted with Hannegan & Associates to
ssist him in discontinuing the Cycle of Hope in his life and suc-
essfully moving through the Healthy Change Process with his
usiness. He was committed to completing the steps necessary to
ncrease interdependency in his personal and professional rela-
ionships. He was eager to start moving past the emotional blocks
hat would otherwise sabotage his business integrity and ultimately
is financial security.

Scott began unraveling the mystery of how he was pro-
rammed in co-dependency by the impact of dysfunction in his
amily and by his position as the oldest son making him respon-
ible for being the family hero.

As he moved through the sadness, guilt and shame that had
een with him since childhood, he began to strengthen his self-
steem. This was reflected in his honest communications, his
bility to establish boundaries and a depth of interdependency in
is personal and professional relationships that he always wanted.

Scott made interdependency a valued part of his life. In his
usiness he demonstrated increased skills in interdependency
nd provided training for his entire staff in order to escort them
hrough the Healthy Change Process. At times, old behaviors
vould recur for Scott and his employees. With practice and
erseverance, he encouraged his staff to continue moving toward
he goal of interdependency and a healthy work environment.
To address the personal lives of his employees, Scott contracted
vith an Employee Assistance Program to provide the counsel-
ng necessary to resolve co-dependent and counterdependent
eliefs and behaviors and to fortify the Healthy Change Process.

Scott was active in AGC and made it a point to network and build interdependent work relationships with its members. He valued every opportunity to prove the quality of his subcontracting services and to build healthy work relationships. The reputation of Benge Construction's quality of performance and commitment to its customers began to spread throughout the Western states. Major contracts started coming to Benge Construction.

A woman construction worker who had been employed by the State of Oregon for several years heard that Benge Construction was "the best" and that people loved to work for Benge. She decided that if she was going to stay in the construction field, she wanted to work for a company that knew how to treat its employees. Scott found the woman sitting on the steps of his office looking quite determined. He asked her what she was doing. She said confidently that she was an excellent worker and wanted to work for the company which took pride in its work and knew how to treat its employees, adding that she was going to sit on the steps no matter how long it took until she was hired and could prove herself. Scott gave her an opportunity and she did prove herself not only to be an excellent worker but also to be in alignment with Scott's vision of developing a healthy organization with an interdependent employee culture.

Benge Construction has grown steadily and is financially secure. The company has a million-dollar credit line which it has not had to use in the last few years. Scott refers to each year of business as "the best year" due to the consistent solid growth.

During an expansion in 1993, Scott demonstrated his commitment to the integrity of his company. Scott, in coordination with his staff, made a commitment to substantial growth. They surpassed their expectations and doubled in size to a $20 million company. While pleased with the successful expansion, Scott and his employees value most the quality of relationship with each other and their customers.

When Scott is asked what is the primary focus of his business, he says, "First relationship with self, then relationship with others." He carries the principle of interdependent relationships to the point that if he is unable to have a healthy interdependent work relationship with a customer he turns down that business, because "The money is not worth tolerating dysfunction."

Scott invests in himself, his employees and his customers in a way that brings the biggest profits—personally and professionally.

A Word to Consultants

A Healthy Approach for Business Consultants

I strongly suggest that consultants in business gain education and training in dysfunctional organizations and co-dependent/counterdependent work relationships.

Without this training, consultants enter the workplace unprepared to effectively deal with the root issue of the symptoms exposed on the surface of the "Iceberg Model" (Chapter 4).

There is a constant backlash of bad press when thousands of dollars have been spent on a consultant and the real issue is not resolved. Many times the criticism is correct, because the consultant works on the symptoms, not the source of the real issue. It is like having a doctor hand you a handkerchief for your cold. It is nice to be able to clean up your face a bit, but it doesn't make the cold go away. There are also many times when a consultant does address the source of the real issue, but members of the organization have no intention of dealing with the cold—they just wanted a handkerchief. At those times consultants who are not astute in dysfunction and co-dependent/

counterdependent behavior are amazed and baffled. This confusion is compounded when the organization blames the consultant for not solving its problem, the one it had no intention of dealing with.

To be an authentic and effective counselor one must first deal with personal dysfunction, addiction and co-dependency/counterdependency. You can't talk it until you walk it. In like manner, to be an authentic and effective consultant, you need to walk it before you talk it. By resolving personal co-dependency/counterdependency issues such as dysfunction and addiction, your professional life will reflect this. What you bring to the organization will be more than just knowledge—it will be a living example of what is possible.

Counselors who have not dealt with their co-dependent beliefs will enable their clients in an unhealthy lifestyle. Consultants who have not dealt with their co-dependent beliefs will enable employees and organizations in dysfunctional behavior.

Consultants will help dysfunctional cycles to continue if they don't take personal responsibility to break their own dysfunctional cycle first.

I have outlined a guideline to help in maintaining a healthy approach to being a consultant. Walking into a dysfunctional organization to perform an intervention is similar to walking into a dysfunctional family to perform an intervention. The power of the dysfunctional system is overwhelming and can neutralize any attempt for change if the professional is not skilled and prepared for the task at hand.

When consulting to an organization:

- Determine what is and is not possible in assisting the organization in becoming more healthy and whole.

- Do not enable the dysfunctional system by being a rescuer.

- Be honest and politically astute.

- Handle all situations ethically.

- Name issues and possible solutions.

- Ask for commitment to change.

- Assist the organization in taking responsibility for implementing its own change.

- Be a neutral committed participant.

- Keep communication open and honest.

- Focus on "What can I contribute to assist this organization to increase organizational health?"

According to an organizational-development principle, if there is a 10 percent change for the better you have done a good job. The ripple effect can also start a chain of events that can increase the percentage of initial change.

Remember: By the organization's *actions* (not words) you will know if it chooses to continue being a dysfunctional system or if it is committed to establishing and maintaining a healthy organization.

When working with an organization, provide the best possible service and recite the serenity prayer to yourself as often as needed:

> *God, grant me the serenity*
> *to accept the things*
> *I cannot change,*
> *the courage to change*
> *the things I can,*
> *and the wisdom to know*
> *the difference.*

Bibliography
and Further Reading

Adams, John D. *Transforming Work*. Alexandria, Va.: Miles River, 1984.

Anderson, Nancy. *Work with Passion: How to Do What You Love for a Living*. New York: Carroll and Graf, 1984.

Beattie, Melody. *Co-dependent No More: How to Stop Controlling Others and Start Caring for Yourself*. New York: Harper/Hazelden, 1987.

Black, Claudia. *It Will Never Happen to Me!* New York: Ballantine, 1981.

Booth, Leo. *When God Becomes a Drug: Breaking the Chains of Religious Addiction and Abuse*. Los Angeles: Tarcher, 1991.

Bradshaw, John. *Bradshaw On: The Family: A Revolutionary Way of Self-Discovery*. Pompano Beach, Fla.: Health Communications, 1988.

Bridges, William. *Job Shift: How to Prosper in a Workplace Without Jobs*. Reading, Mass.: Addison-Wesley, 1994.

Bridges, William. *Transitions: Making Sense of Life's Changes*. Reading, Mass.: Addison-Wesley, 1980.

Cooper, Cary L. *The Stress Check: Coping with the Stresses of Life and Work*. Englewood Cliffs, N.J.: Prentice-Hall, 1981.

Covey, Stephen R. *The Seven Habits of Highly Effective People: Restoring the Character Ethic*. New York: Simon and Schuster, 1989.

Depree, Max. *Leadership Is an Art*. New York: Doubleday, 1989.

Dominguez, Joseph, and Vicki Robin. *Your Money or Your Life: Transforming Your Relationship with Money and Achieving Financial Independence*. New York: Viking, 1992.

Falkenstein, Lynda. *Niche Craft: The Art of Being Special*. Portland Ore.: Niche Presse, 1990.

Foster, Carolyn. *Family Patterns Workbook: Breaking Free from Your Past and Creating a Life of Your Own*. New York: Tarcher Perigree 1993.

Fox, Matthew. *The Reinvention of Work: A New Vision of Livelihood for Our Time*. San Francisco: HarperSanFrancisco, 1994.

Fritz, Robert. *The Path of Least Resistance: Learning to Become the Creative Force in Your Own Life*. New York: Fawcett, 1989.

Gawain, Shakti. *The Path of Transformation: How Healing Ourselves Can Change the World*. Mill Valley, Calif.: Nataraj, 1993.

Hammer, Michael, and James Champy. *Reengineering the Corporations: A Manifesto for Business Revolution*. New York: Harper Business, 1993.

Jaffe, Dennis T. *Take This Job and Love It: How to Change Your Work Without Changing Your Job*. New York: Simon and Schuster, 1988.

Jeffers, Susan. *Feel the Fear and Do It Anyway*. San Diego, Calif.: Harcourt Brace Jovanovich, 1987.

Kanter, Rosa Beth Moss. *When Giants Learn to Dance: Mastering the Challenges of Strategy, Management and Careers in the 1990s*. New York: Simon and Schuster, 1989.

Lipnack, Jessica. *The Networking Book: People Connecting with People*. New York: Viking Penguin, 1988.

London, Manuel. *Career Management and Survival in the Workplace: Helping Employees Make Tough Career Decisions, Stay Motivated, and Reduce Career Stress*. San Francisco: Jossey-Bass, 1987.

Millman, Dan. *The Life You Were Born to Live: A Guide to Finding Your Life Purpose*. Tiburon, Calif.: H.J. Kramer, 1993.

Naisbitt, John, and Patricia Aburdene. *Re-Inventing the Corporation*. New York: Warner, 1986.

Nelson, Bob. *1001 Ways to Reward Employees*. New York: Workman 1993.

Palazzoli, Mara Selvini. *The Hidden Games of Organizations*. New York: Pantheon, 1986.

Peck, M. Scott. *The Road Less Traveled: A New Psychology of Love, Traditional Values and Spiritual Growth*. New York: Simon and Schuster, 1978.

Peters, Tom. *Thriving on Chaos: A Handbook for Management Revolution*. New York: Knopf, 1987.

Robbins, Stephen P. *Organizational Behavior: Concepts, Controversies, and Applications*. Englewood Cliffs, N.J.: Prentice-Hall, 1992.

Robinson, Bryan E. *Work Addiction: Hidden Legacies of Adult Children*. Deerfield Beach, Fla.: Health Communications, 1989.

Saltzman, Amy. *Downshifting: Reinventing Success on a Slower Track*. New York: HarperCollins, 1991.

Schaef, Anne Wilson. *Co-Dependence: Misunderstood-Mistreated*. San Francisco: HarperSanFrancisco, 1992.

Schaef, Anne Wilson, and Diane Fassel. *The Addictive Organization: Why We Overwork, Cover Up, Pick Up the Pieces, Please the Boss, and Perpetuate Sick Organizations*. San Francisco: HarperSanFrancisco, 1990.

Sher, Barbara. *WishCraft: How to Get What You Really Want*. New York: Viking, 1979.

Sprankle, Judith, and Henry Ebel. *The Workaholic Syndrome*. New York: Walker, 1987.

Subby, Robert. *Lost in the Shuffle: The Co-dependent Reality*. Pompano Beach, Fla.: Health Communications, 1987.

Walton, Richard E. *Interpersonal Peacemaking: Confrontations and Third-party Consultation*. Reading, Mass.: Addison-Wesley, 1969.

Wegscheider-Cruse, Sharon. *Choicemaking: For Co-dependents, Adult Children, and Spirituality Seekers*. Deerfield Beach, Fla.: Health Communications, 1985.

Wegscheider-Cruse, Sharon. *Learning to Love Yourself: Finding Your Self-Worth*. Deerfield Beach, Fla.: Health Communications, 1987.

Whyte, David. *Heart Aroused: Poetry and the Preservation of the Soul in Corporate America*. New York: Currency Doubleday, 1994.

Woititz, Janet. *Home Away from Home*. Pompano Beach, Fla.: Health Communications, 1987.

About the Author

Eileen R. Hannegan, M.S., a counselor and business consultant, operates her firm, Hannegan & Associates, in the Portland, Oregon, area.

She specializes in assisting professionals and organizations through the Healthy Change Process.

Ms. Hannegan is a national trainer and speaker at conferences, universities, hospitals, organizations and community associations on the topic of "Creating Healthy Organizations and Interdependent Employee Cultures."

Beyond Words Publishing, Inc.

Our corporate mission:
"Inspire to Integrity"

Our declared values:

- ▲ We give to all of life as life has given us.
- ▲ We honor all relationships.
- ▲ Trust and stewardship are integral to fulfilling dreams.
- ▲ Collaboration is essential to create miracles.
- ▲ Creativity and aesthetics nourish the soul.
- ▲ Unlimited thinking is fundamental.
- ▲ Living your passion is vital.
- ▲ Joy and humor open our hearts to growth.
- ▲ It is important to remind ourselves of love.

Our promise to our customers:

We will provide you with the highest quality books and related products that meet or exceed your expectations. As our customer, you will be satisfied with your purchase and will receive your order promptly, or we will refund your money.

To order or to receive a catalog, contact:
Beyond Words Publishing, Inc.
4443 NE Airport Road
Hillsboro, Oregon 97124
503-693-8700 or 1-800-284-9673

Other Titles
from Beyond Words Publishing, Inc.'s
The Business of Life Series

YOU CAN HAVE IT ALL
by Arnold M. Patent, $18.95 hardcover

Joy, peace, abundance—these gifts of the Universe are available to each of us whenever we choose to play the *real* game of life: the game of mutual support. *You Can Have It All* is a guidebook that shows us how to move beyond our beliefs in struggle and shortage, open our hearts, and enjoy a life of true ecstasy. Arnold Patent first self-published *You Can Have It All* in 1984, and it became a self-publishing classic with over 200,000 copies in print. This revised and expanded edition reflects his greater understanding of the principles and offers practical suggestions as well as simple exercises for improving the quality of our lives.

THE WOMAN'S BOOK OF CREATIVITY
by C Diane Ealy, Ph.D., $12.95 softcover

The ability to express the self creatively is a foundation for greater joy and satisfaction. *The Woman's Book of Creativity* taps into the creative energies of women and considers how a woman's thought process is particularly conducive to creativity. C Diane Ealy, Ph.D., writes that creativity is a natural outgrowth of being human, not limited to the arts, but demonstrated in the activities we undertake every day. The book offers activities and insights that assist in enhancing a woman's creative process.

THE VENTURE ADVENTURE:
Strategies for Thriving in the Jungle of Entrepreneurship
by Daryl Bernstein, $18.95 hardcover, $12.95 softcover

Daryl Bernstein, who has been enjoying business success since he was eight years old, makes the entrepreneurial spirit approachable to anyone with *The Venture Adventure*. Now the idea of self-employment becomes an exciting world of possibility. Bernstein teaches the reader how to recognize landmark ideas, how to create profitable, useful services, and how to use follow-up strategies to ensure a venture's long-term success. The ideas are useful for anyone considering starting a business and are aimed specifically at those looking for alternatives to stepping onto the corporate ladder.

HINDSIGHTS:
The Wisdom and Breakthroughs of Remarkable People
by Guy Kawasaki, $22.95 hardcover

What have you learned from your life that you would like to share with the next generation? Get a fresh appreciation of the human experience in this inspirational collection of interviews with thirty-three people who have overcome unique challenges. They are candid about their failures and disappointments, and insightful about turning adversity into opportunity. Guy Kawasaki spent over two years researching and interviewing such people as Apple Computer co-founder Steve Wozniak, management guru Tom Peters, and entrepreneur Mary Kay. But not everyone in the book is a celebrity. They share their revelations and life experiences, motivating the reader for both personal and professional growth.